ESSAYS AND STUDIES
1963

ESSAYS AND STUDIES
1963

BEING VOLUME SIXTEEN OF THE NEW SERIES
OF ESSAYS AND STUDIES COLLECTED FOR
THE ENGLISH ASSOCIATION
BY S. GORLEY PUTT

JOHN MURRAY
FIFTY ALBEMARLE STREET LONDON

Contents

I

On Publishing

MILTON WALDMAN

AT one end of the process is the writer, at the other the reader. Of both there are various sorts. There is the writer (commonly known as the author) who sets down his thoughts, fancies and knowledge for the purpose of selling them; there is also the compiler (contractually often known as the editor) of works of reference, manuals, almanacs, statistical tables, etc. Where the book is mainly or largely composed of pictures the photographer or illustrator stands to it in somewhat the same relation. Between readers there are differences equally marked. Some read to nourish the mind or the imagination, to stimulate or soothe the nerves, some consult for more directly practical purposes; while—to alter the categories—some exercise their choice in the buying or borrowing of reading matter, others take what they are given or ordered to acquire, at their own or other's expense, as in the case of text-books. The function of the publisher, his endeavour and interest, is to serve as middleman between writers and readers of whatever category.

This has always been his function, whether, as in earlier times, as printer or bookseller, whether subsidized directly by the writer or indirectly by the writer's patron. The fact stands out more clearly now that he is commonly neither printer nor bookseller but the employer of the one and the supplier of the other. It is he who decides what the printer shall print and the bookseller sell, in what form and quantity and (so long as the Net Book Agreement stands) at what price the writer's work shall be made available to the reader. The writer stands in need not only of financial but editorial assistance before his manuscript is completed, not seldom before it is even begun; the finished text must be examined for literal or factual accuracy; type, paper and binding studied in relation to comeliness and economy, the ensuing decisions delivered along with the manuscript to the selected printer for transformation into a book, or rather books, to a number based upon the attempt to evaluate quality in terms of quantity; in other words, to anticipate demand. Advertising and publicity have meanwhile to be prepared, press and wireless to be advised and bookshops canvassed so that when the book emerges its merits will have been sufficiently recognized to bring the public into the shops. Thereafter if successful it has to be 'nursed' by further publicity, advertising and intensive selling, the stock carefully watched so that reprints may be ready in time to meet re-orders. It is hard to see how, without publishers to undertake and finance these various operations, the production and circulation of books would in modern times have been possible.

But of course times do not remain modern; by the time they are identified as being so they very likely no longer are. The foregoing description of a publisher's activities is in general as applicable to 1900 as to 1963; what has changed within that period is the differentiation in character between one publisher and another. During much of the nineteenth century and the early part of the twentieth an imprint commonly reflected the personal preference of its proprietor. If he liked what a writer had to say and the way he said it, that writer's books were made welcome to his list; if not, external considerations, whether of reputation or money, were unlikely to alter his opinion that their proper place was elsewhere, or nowhere. Moreover the books of his choice displayed to the eye as well as the mind the idiosyncrasies of his taste: their physical appearance proclaimed their origin as unmistakably as the trademark or 'colophon'. Messrs. John Lane, Martin Secker, Grant Richards, Smith Elder and their similars not only published the works of Wilde, Beardsley, Saki, Beerbohm, Firbank and their contemporaries, they became identified with them, created for themselves something resembling what would now be called a 'brand image'. It may have no significance that the publishers named eventually confronted insolvency, but I fear that the fact is more than co-incidental.

Not that the creation of the individual image ceased or inevitably led to disaster. In the years between the wars few experienced readers, regarding an assortment of books in a shop with the publishers' names blanked out, would have gone far wrong in differentiating Cape's from Chatto's or Gollancz's (though in the case of Gollancz, as formerly in that of Lane, it would have been a disadvantage to be colour-blind in respect of yellow). Even today a Penguin or an A. and C. Black volume of reference or a Phaidon art book has contrived to achieve something of the collective individuality pertaining to the concept of the brand image. But these are already exceptions to the rule, and would be even if the rule still prevailed, paperbacks necessarily covering too wide, reference and art books too narrow a field to be altogether typical of it. Inexorably, for reasons now to be considered, the tendency has been for the publisher's output to proliferate, his activities to multiply not only in size but in kind, until the cultivation of a list based upon personal preference has become all but impossible.

The most obvious of the reasons is, as one might expect, economic, but this in turn derives from more profound factors of social change. Not much more than a generation ago it would have been possible to found a small publishing business with a capital of £10,000—a sum not beyond the reach of a fairly large number of young men with an inclination towards books, some practical experience and a prosperous father or friend. If the business thrived it should after two or three years have been capable of turning the original capital over something like three times annually. If it did, and was efficiently managed, the annual profit available for distribution to the owner or owners should have been in the neighbourhood of £5,000—quite a respectable income for the time even when divided between two. To attain it no more than twenty or thirty new books and reprints a year would have been necessary, assuming that printing quantities had been wisely judged; with ordinary luck the inevitable failures would have been balanced by the occasional best-sellers, and the business over the years might hope to build up a sound back list and a reasonable degree of stability.

This is still the dream of many a man who feels the call to become a publisher, but he is unlikely to realize it. He may have the best training, sound and even original ideas about the production and promoting of books, an ability to get on with authors, a flair for imparting a definite character to his list. He may even have access to the £50,000 now deemed the bare—the niggardly—minimum required to establish a new imprint. The chances are that he will sooner or later have to merge with or sell out to somebody else. In either event he will have diluted or parted with his individuality as a publisher.

The tendency to merger or absorption is, of course characteristic of our time and affects virtually all branches of commerce and industry. The costs, particularly the labour costs, in relation to the selling price of any given article or transaction have tended steadily to rise, the margin of profit to decrease. The solution has generally taken the form of reducing the cost of the individual operation by technical improvement and spreading the overall cost over a larger volume of business; this necessitates both the introduction of substantial sums of capital and the elimination or restraint of wasteful competition. All these considerations apply to publishing, but within limits and subject to refinements and qualifications due to its peculiar nature.

For publishing can neither command its raw material, of which by far the largest and most characteristic part originates in the human brain, nor indefinitely extend the market for its end-product, which must satisfy an infinite diversity of tastes and needs. The whole of it can never be anything but a small industry producing a vast assortment of small, comparatively low-priced, non-interchangeable but hardly indispensable articles. Its total volume of business this year is unlikely to exceed £65,000,000, its output to fall below 22,000 separate titles inclusive of a relatively small number of old ones brought back into print—a gross income within the range of a single unified industry producing a fraction of a per cent of the variety of merchandise, and moreover producing it with little or no modification year after year. Plainly a properly rationalized book trade would strive to produce fewer books bringing in more money. It is an unattainable ideal for the reason that there is no certainty beforehand which of the books the public will buy and very considerable probability that it will not pay more for them even if it has to go without. Of both statements the history of publishing offers strong empirical proof.

As I have said, the publisher cannot command his raw material. It does not, like most raw material, come directly or indirectly out of the ground; there is little to be done in the way of stimulating or restricting its output according to the state of the market. The publisher must choose from what comes to him; there is no more to be made from no books than from unsatisfactory books, and if the overheads are to be met some books he must have. Authors he has published before, especially if they are already established, present no problem. But they may die, go off form or go elsewhere; the gaps must be filled, and more, if he is to keep up and meet necessary increases of salary, etc. His readers recommend a manuscript displaying some of the characteristics of a recent best-seller. The *gros publique* is known to like the same thing over and over, but may they not have had enough of this particular thing? Another manuscript is submitted which shows evidences of striking originality. It seems doubtful many will understand it: on the other hand may it not be the sensational novelty of which every publisher dreams, the work of literature which will be the book of the season or the year? With either offering there is always the possibility that a rival will take it and make a good thing of it. In the end, by guess-work, flair, intuition, absent-mindedness and sheer desperation enough is available upon which to predicate a list for the next season but one. By the use of the same intellectual and emotional devices a number is arrived at denoting each title's original expectation of sale and inserted into the instructions accompanying the manuscript to the printer.

This drama is, and doubtless long has been, acted out in every publisher's office. Whether it will have a happy ending or not must await determination in the bookshops. But to this uncertainty there is one exception already suggested, the established author with a dependable record of sales, with whom should be joined the non-professional writer, the established public figure, whether politician, soldier, diplomat or explorer, with a personal story to tell which many are eager to hear. These are the backbone of the list: and the incidence of their distribution is central to the question why larger publishers tend to grow larger and smaller to be driven to shelter lest they disappear altogether. Authors in general tend to be loyal to those who first gave them their chance, and publishers to refrain from enticing them away. But temptation can grow to such a size that it alters not only in degree but in kind, and renders the old-fashioned loyalty not only difficult but irrelevant.

For along with the tendency to alliance and absorption within the publishing trade have arisen forces outside it which irresistibly draw or drive it to dependence on larger entities—the entertainment industry on one side and government on another. Just as the small, selective publisher is finding it difficult to survive owing to rising costs and smaller profit margins, so the trade as a whole can no longer be certain of maintaining itself by providing books to the reading public. A large and increasing proportion of publishers' profits is now derived not from the sale of books but of rights to the use of the material in them: by films, television, wireless, by magazines in serial or digest form, for translation into foreign languages. The value of such rights on their present scale is so recent that before the war publishers sometimes disregarded them in their contracts with their authors. Then much the most valuable 'subsidiary' (as they are still called) consisted in the sale of licence or a special edition of many thousands of copies to a book club which issued the title under its own imprint.[1] Today the book clubs, though still important, command nothing like the membership they once did either in Great Britain or the United States. But alongside and to an extent replacing them as outlets for large quantities of books have sprung up the paperback publishers, who offer sums varying from a few hundred to a great many thousands of pounds for the right to print and distribute titles held in copyright by others.

The rapid increase in the value of these various rights has con-

[1] I am ignoring the hard-cover reprint houses, which never flourished in Great Britain as they did in the U.S.

siderably affected the position of the publisher as middleman. For he now mediates not only between the author and the reader but, on quite other terms, between the author and large organizations dealing in mass entertainment or, in the case of the magazine and the paperback, mass inexpensive reading matter. His income is derived not only from the sale of a few or a few hundred copies at a pre-determined price, but of rights separately negotiated at a highly variable price. The author and his agent—a highly important figure—are not unaware of these potentialities; and with the established author, at least, the original contract has to be negotiated with them in mind. Thirty years ago an advance against royalties of £1,000 would have been regarded as substantial. Today advances of £10,000 are not uncommon, of £50,000 or more by no means unheard of: for both parties to the contract calculate that the sum will be secured not alone by the sale of X number of copies but by the total to be derived from the sale of the subsidiary rights, of which the publisher's share is either fixed by custom or separately negotiated beforehand. The ability to undertake such contracts demands on the part of the buyer considerable resources of cash and credit, as well as a considerable organization to distribute books in the quantities envisaged at home and overseas and to undertake the manifold and complicated external relations involved. The author, or more likely his agent, with a book of such calibre to offer, is obviously more likely to offer it to a big publisher than a little one.

Moreover it is not only the author or his agent who is likely to approach the larger publisher, but also the purchaser of rights. His demands are incessant for material that will make successful films, serials, digests or paperback editions. He cannot lie back and wait for only what is offered; he must take the initiative in inventing and procuring what he requires. By way of studio and editorial conferences, observation of current tastes and market research he has discovered it: a best-selling book of a certain sort or on a given subject capable of being adapted to his medium or capable of circulating in paperback in hundreds of thousands or millions. He has little or no direct contact with the author likely to produce the sort of book he wants; for an actual book in hard

B

cover is ordinarily considered the best way to test the public's reaction and set the whole thing going. So he makes a proposal to a publisher, who if he is interested makes another to the author or his agent. The first proposal may very likely suggest a scale of payments—so much if the hard cover edition sells 50,000, so much more if 75,000 and so on. An offer may be included to subsidize the advertising, but the publisher, if he is to reach the figures mentioned, must reckon on his own considerable outlays for the purpose. Again the operation is mounted on such a scale as in general to concern only the larger publishers—who, moreover, are more likely to have under contract the kind of author desired.

It is hard to see how the tendency here described can be arrested, let alone reversed. The public appetite for general literature, even on a popular level, is not insatiable. The price of books has risen, but less than the general level of prices—not more than double for ordinary novels or works of non-fiction since before the war. One sufferer from the disparity has been the author who has no great expectation—and comparatively few have—from the sale of subsidiary rights. Before the war the well-established could hope for a royalty of 25 per cent; a little over a hundred years ago Macaulay received $33\frac{1}{3}$ per cent on a guinea volume. Today 20 per cent is the maximum, accorded to a comparative few; $17\frac{1}{2}$ per cent is more usually the limit, and only after the sale of some thousands of copies calculated at a smaller percentage. The proportion of overseas sales to the total has risen sharply, and upon these, owing to the higher rate of discount allowed, the royalty is calculated at 5 per cent or $6\frac{1}{2}$ per cent. So even if there were an indefinitely expanding market the author's gross income from the sales of his books alone has a hard time keeping pace with the general cost of living. Yet in the same period the rise in the rate of income tax has widened the gap between gross and expendable income, so that considerably increased earnings are necessary to maintain the latter at an adequate, stable figure. This is all the more true in a profession where one may earn large sums from a best-seller in one year and very little for several years thereafter. The distinguished public figure, on the other hand, who writes one book and may never write another, is likely to demand an outright capital sum amounting to all anticipated earnings because this may be allowed him free of tax and be placed in a trust for the benefit of his heirs—another reason for this type of book usually appearing under the imprint of one of the larger publishers.

There are analagous problems from the publisher's side and their solution has led to some interesting consequences. The bookshops, the traditional outlet for books of general interest, complain, with reason, that they cannot survive on the discounts allowed them; the publishers allege, also with reason, that the margin of profit on a book is insufficient for them to allow more. The result is that many bookshops, even old-established ones, have given up and few new ones are being started. The wholesalers, whose large pre-publication orders were once regarded as indispensable to the success of a book, have virtually disappeared; the commercial libraries, formerly a most important channel for the circulation of new books, are a vanishing institution. If the Net Book Agreement, by which the bookseller is assured of receiving the full retail price of a new volume, is abolished the process will be accelerated, as books may well be undersold, be made 'loss leaders' by the big stores. Other outlets are being sought, such as sales to the customer by direct mail order, but these are still in their experimental stage and their possible effect on the remaining bookshops at the least uncertain. With other articles increased popular demand is often achieved by high-powered advertising, but it seems ill-adapted to books because of their very nature. For with those other articles to promote one is to promote all in its category. To urge the public to buy a certain brand of beer helps to make it conscious of beer as a desirable beverage: other brands will profit. So much is this true that growers and producers often pool their resources in an advertising campaign which merely reiterates 'Buy Apples' 'or 'Drink More Milk'. But one crate of apples or one bottle of milk is more likely to resemble and therefore serve as a substitute for another than are any books. Advertising may—experience shows that it does not inevitably—increase the demand for a particular book, but if it does it may well be at the expense rather than for the benefit of another. One can hardly imagine going into a shop and ordering a book impelled merely by the appeal on a thousand hoardings 'Buy More Books'. Even authors, to please whom is the motive of much of a publisher's advertising, would take a dim view of such unselective expenditure.

A consistent and continuing expansion, normally considered indispensable to a healthy trade or industry—'Go up or go down' —seems therefore not within the purview of general publishing. Individual publishers may grow as the result of good management and good luck, but the trade as a whole seems to be circumscribed unless and until some way is found to enlarge the absorptive capacity of the reading public. Mergers and acquisitions may effect certain economies within the firm or group, but even these are limited by the fact that each title must receive individual production and promotion. The survivors of the competition remain in competition: it is no solution for fewer publishers to offer annually more books to an insufficiently increasing number of buyers.

Where the solution does at present appear to lie is in the 'captive buyer', namely the recipient of education whose reading is either required or subsidized by public authority. There are few general publishers, however successful in their own field, who are not casting wistful eyes on this vast, growing and apparently inexhaustible market. More positive information can be obtained, from examination school boards, teachers etc., about the response to be anticipated from potential consumers than can be obtained from any source about that of the wider public to novels, histories, biographies or tales of adventure; quantities can be predicted in advance without the waste of under- or over-printing; production and promotion reduced to the simplest methods. Of course special editorial and selling departments have to be set up, but once they are smoothly operating one knows where one is, not only from year to year but over a period of years. Whatever the political future may be, the English language will remain the chief medium of communication over wide areas of the world. In them, in the education of their populations, obviously lies much of the future of British book publishing. And not only of British but of American, to judge by the eagerness of American publishers to buy British firms in order to gain legal access to the market.

All this means greater concentration, larger units, greater specialization within the units, rule by technicians rather than owners—as in most other forms of business. The same rule applies because that is what publishing is, a business. Of itself it cannot pretend to create literature or add to knowledge; it can only foster them by such aid as it can give to those who produce them and by making them as widely available as possible to those who seek them. But this, one may safely say, it will always do, under whatever form of organization, not only out of self-interest but the desire to do so. For even the technician, more particularly the editorial technician, will always take delight in discovering the original artist or scholar and introducing him to a world which can never have enough of either.

II

The Fascination of the Paranoid Personality:
Baron Corvo[1]

PAMELA HANSFORD JOHNSON

'REMEMBER that people who feel persecuted have usually something to feel persecuted about.' To a paranoid personality, like Rolfe's, a single injury is fertile as a dandelion head, scattering its energetic seeds over the whole of a life. Who knows what seed gave birth to that particular dandelion? But there must have been a seed, must have been a wrong.

The paranoiac, feeling—in fact, knowing—the hand of all men against him, takes the perfectly normal course towards enemy hands: he bites them. And innocent hands bleed with the guilty. He is very strong, he is very sure of himself, injustice is the beacon burning in his head. He attracts by his strength and by his heat, wins admiration by the very selflessness of his mania. For with men like Rolfe, the mania *is* selfless: they want justice, admiration, fame, not for themselves but in acknowledgment of what they *are*, of their native gifts, God-given—in recognition of which they are always in an interior state of humble and bewildered gratitude. The moment a man thinks he cannot conceivably be wrong, he is in a very powerful position with regard to those not naturally resistant to this kind of thinking. It never entered Rolfe's head that any fault could possibly lie with himself. I doubt if it entered Savonarola's.

Paranoia and great courage, moral and physical, often go together; and courage is alluring in itself. The man who doesn't

[1] This essay, forming the introduction to *Corvo, 1860–1960*, a limited edition of essays by various hands published by the St. Albert's Press, Aylesford, to commemorate the centenary of the birth of Fr. Rolfe, Baron Corvo, is reprinted by kind permission of the editors, Mr. Cecil Woolf and Fr. Brocard Sewell.

give a damn, how we admire him, wish we were like him! The man who is sure enough of himself to rend others with his savagery, his sarcasm, his brutal truthfulness—we have only to consider the response to the comedy of the Marx Brothers, who were able to release, vicariously, the social bonds of the personality. Savonarola, Rolfe, the stage-*persona* of Groucho Marx: there is something in common.

When I try to analyse for myself why Rolfe was so fascinating to me that I used him as a starting-point for the hero of one of my own novels, I can disentangle three elements, though I still do not know which of them is the dominant one. First, perhaps he appeals to a paranoid streak in my own nature (which few writers are without, to a greater or lesser extent). I, too, would like to bite a few hands on occasion; I, too, would like to snarl, to deride, to insult. I suppose I would: I do not really indulge in these things, but I feel a dreadful glee when Rolfe does them for me. I am in complete agreement with Dr. Bertram Korn that he may mirror for us some of our buried desires. Second, though it runs hard against my sympathies intellectually, I am moved by the spectacle of the absolute self-dedication of the artist. Rolfe had, as has been said, no talent, but a little genius. He felt himself, knew himself, all genius. He would have starved for it, and he did. He would have died for it. In the end perhaps he did. Third, I am mesmerized by the brute physical courage that kept him going through the Venetian winters: if anyone wants to know what it is like to sleep out on those bitter waters in January, Rolfe will give him an account to make the heart and the bones ache.

Yet I am fascinated by him rather as a character in fiction than as a man who really lived and breathed. I should be less than honest if I did not say that I think he was pretty mad. I think he was one of the few paranoid personalities in whom silliness transcends itself into the purely terrible. I do not think the Venice letters can be written off as easily as some would like— neither for good nor ill. For there really is something splendid, almost mythological, about their ramping sexuality; it was so extremely whole-hearted, as everything about him was. If one must read this kind of thing, Rolfe is incomparably better at it than Henry Miller. And there are a few passages of descriptive splendour as fine as any in *The Desire and Pursuit of the Whole*, where the physical beauty of Venice is expressed as no one else ever did it, before Rolfe or after him.

Yet he had fallen into a disease of the spirit so gross, so monstrous, that I really cannot believe all this would have been quite different if he had been given charge of an obscure parish. (I can't help feeling that it wouldn't have remained obscure for long.) I do not say this, remember, as I would say it about a real man; I am making my comments as if Rolfe were one of man's great creations, like the Baron de Charlus.

Of the reality of his vocation I have no right to speak, except in judging him as I would a character in a major novel. I suspect that he wanted less to be priest than to be Pope. He had the *folie de grandeur* in all its magnificence. He reminds me, again and again, of that frightful parable in the Brothers Grimm about the magic flounder, who satisfied all the increasingly rapacious desires of the poor fisherman's wife—to live in a palace, to be Queen, to be Emperor, to be Pope—until she overplayed her hand and demanded that he should make her Ruler of the Universe. The flounder rose for the last time out of a pitch-black hurricane. 'Go back,' he cried to the hen-pecked, Emperor-pecked, Pope-pecked husband, 'and find her back in her wretched hovel.' Poor Rolfe found himself back in his *pupparin*, in the wet and windy Venetian night.

I am sure he had some cause for paranoia: he was shabbily treated by R. H. Benson, and by some others. But there is a converse to the dictum with which I began my note, and it is this: 'Remember that people who feel persecuted have usually done something to be persecuted for.' Perhaps not much: but something. And perhaps a great deal. I think no one can read Victor Hall's account of the rise and fall of the friendship between Mrs. van Someren, her husband and Rolfe, without feeling that hers is the word to accept.

The paranoid personality very often has the power to give a significant, penetrating quality to literary expression. This can be very clear and brilliant, as in the case of Rolfe, clear and heavy, as in the case of Martin Luther, or insistent and turgid, as in the case of Hitler: but the quality is much the same. It is surprisingly easy when reading Rolfe to accept him on his own valuation: to accept even the screams of revenge, of abuse, of denunciation. One feels there must be something in it.

And of course, there is: there is black tragedy in it, his personal tragedy, none the less to him because it was so largely self-wrought. *The Desire and Pursuit of the Whole, Hadrian the Seventh, Nicholas Crabbe*, they are very tragical mirth, hot ice, and wondrous strange snow. In the world of his own creation, he is very much the hero: so much so, that all the rest are the merest supporting players. No one can stand up to him. The terrible little man towers a mile high out of the desert of his own life.

I am not sentimental enough to think that had Rolfe and I known each other, we should have rubbed along nicely; to think that I might have been the one person to understand him; mine the hand to remain unbitten. His English friends in Venice seem to me to have been marvels of patience; I should not have done half so well as they. Yet, with a year between my birth and his death, I feel safe in admitting his attraction for me. Like most paranoiacs, he achieves a real touch of splendour.

Falling into the canal and emerging with pipe still in his mouth: in full cardinal's rig chasing poor Lady Layard's funeral gondola up the Grand Canal and howling abuse (if this story is not apocryphal): haughty and starving, attending a party for the sake of the cocktail titbits: huddling in his leaky boat, under tarpaulins, in the black rage of winter and noting still, that 'The lengthy line of lights along Spinalonga fluttered like little pale daffodils in a night-mist coloured like the bloom on the fruit of the vine': he is larger than life, much, much larger, and we have found him larger than death.

III

The Hawthorne Myth: A Protest

MARTIN GREEN

I

HAWTHORNE'S reputation remains very high in America. In the last ten years at least seven book-length studies have appeared (with authors as distinguished as Marius Bewley and Harry Levin) which all present him as a moulder and hero of the modern sensibility. They differ in details of their interpretation, but there is on the whole a remarkable critical unanimity about their view of Hawthorne's work as an allegorical articulation of the deepest and darkest experience of the American psyche. It is still, however, possible to take the view that the critics are inventing meanings for their texts and that Hawthorne's own account of his work is shrewder than theirs.

Hawthorne called his longer works of fiction romances, and his shorter ones tales or sketches, and he defined his sense of those terms:

> The sketches are not, it is hardly necessary to say, profound. . . . They never need translation. . . . They are not the talk of a secluded man with his own mind and heart (had it been so, they could hardly have failed to be more deeply and permanently valuable), but his attempts, and very imperfectly successful ones, to open an intercourse with the world.

This comes from Hawthorne's preface to the third edition of *Twice Told Tales*; a collection which includes 'Young Goodman Brown'. None of Hawthorne's critics has failed to praise his judgement of his own work; but they have all assumed such remarks to be not the modifications of modesty, but a flat contradiction of the truth. They have insisted that the sketches fall into a quite opposite category; that they are 'profound', that they always need translation, that they *are* a dialogue with his own mind and heart, and *not* a performance as clubman-author.

The Preface to *The House of the Seven Gables* begins:

> When a writer calls his work a Romance, it need hardly be observed that he wishes to claim a certain latitude, both as to its fashion and material, which he would not have felt himself entitled to assume, had he professed to be writing a Novel.

This latitude is a freedom from the rigorous discipline of realism, and a freedom in the management of 'his atmospherical medium'; a freedom to 'bring out or mellow the lights, and deepen and enrich the shadows, of the picture'. The device he has most in mind, it appears, is 'the Marvellous'; ghosts, curses, legends, superstitions, omens, etc. The romance writer will not ask his reader to believe in these things; he will be wise, no doubt, 'to mingle the Marvellous rather as a slight, delicate, and evanescent flavour ...' He will describe the superstition, that is, dismiss it laughingly, and then give a hint that perhaps something uncanny really did happen; and isn't it anyway rather nice to think it did. He will not ask us to believe in anything supernatural, or make it 'any portion of the actual substance of the dish offered to the public'. In all this, as he himself observes, Hawthorne is describing a genre with which the readers of 1851 were very familiar. In calling his book a romance and not a novel, he is promising them something in the manner of Mrs. Radcliffe and her successors. That, moreover, is what he gave them. *The House of the Seven Gables, The Scarlet Letter, The Marble Faun, The Blithedale Romance,* are romances in that sense. They differ from novels just in the thinness of their psychological and sociological detail, in their fascination with the supernatural, in the liberties they take with their own verisimilitude; their essential meaning lies in the author's *persona*, in his comments as he conjures up before us, and then dispels, various quaint, gloomy, or charming scenes.

The critics, however, insist that Hawthorne has his own conception of the romance, quite different from Mrs. Radcliffe's; that for him it was a form in which the psychological aspects of spiritual experience could be symbolically rendered. First of all, it is unlikely that any writer could do that without being conscious of it; without in fact saying something about it, in notebook or journal if not in conversation. This is a complex aesthetic strategy; not the sort of thing that gets done unconsciously. Hawthorne made copious notes for and about his own writing; but they contain no hint that he thought of writing anything but the tales and romances he defined in his prefaces. Secondly, Hawthorne in particular was not an intellectual writer in any sense. James remarks several times on how empty of ideas the Journals are, and there is every evidence that Hawthorne never took part in a conversation about ideas or forms in his life. He spent a lot of time in solitary meditation, but he described this as musing or dreaming, and the evidence supports him. Irritated by the intellectual enthusiasm of his Concord neighbours, Hawthorne's recourse was not to a profounder understanding of the American experience, but to the great established truths of the popular heart: Christianity, marriage, democracy.

II

No one, of course, can read Hawthorne without realizing that there is something very different and very deep below the surface. As he makes his comments and invokes his pieties, his voice moves in and out of disturbing echoes produced by a hollow cavity below, quite thinly iced over. But one can feel that Hawthorne gave those depths no voice of their own; that they remained only a distorting and ominous echo. In fact, though they constitute the prime interest of his work for us now, they probably spoiled it for his readers then; they probably prevented him from doing well the kind of writing he was aiming at.

To explain this reading of Hawthorne, it is simplest to refer directly to the facts of his life. His father died while he was a child, his mother withdrew from the world, and his sisters treated him as the most important member of the family. A very handsome, sensitive boy, much petted by them and by his aunts and uncles, and invited into solitude both by the decline of the family fortunes and by his own illness, he seems to have drifted away from normal contacts into a dreamland of stories, totally unchallenged, unaroused, knowing no equals.

At Bowdoin he cultivated the less perceptive, less dangerous companions. 'He would sit for a whole evening with head gently inclined to one side, hearing every word, seeing every gesture, and yet scarcely a word would pass his lips . . . He lives in a mysterious world of thought and imagination which he never permits me to enter.' Cilley assumed that since his friend did not live fully in the normal world of people and things, then he must live in the world of thought and imagination. But Hawthorne tells us over and over that a man may live in neither, may refuse fruitful reciprocation with any aspect of reality. And all the details of Cilley's account confirm Hawthorne's diagnosis; the silence, the watchfulness, the head on one side, the physical clumsiness, the hours of dreaming, the shyness and the lethargy.

Then came twelve appalling years at Salem. Mark van Doren may think them a period of hard work, relieved by diversions and friendships, punctuated by the excitement of artistic accomplishment. Hawthorne was appalled by them. He sat alone in his room all day and night for twelve years; he even sent his sister to the library for him, and only went out himself after dark; he read without studying, mused without thinking, and wrote fanciful, unreal, little sketches. He watched people in the streets and made up stories about them, but refused to meet them socially. Such behaviour could seem, in the 1830's, typical of a writer, and even distinguished, though eccentric. But when he found that his stories were malicious, that they invaded the other person's most sacred privacy, that they were not at all as warm and kindly as, for instance, Dickens's stories, then he felt guilty and frightened. He made great efforts to come out into the world and 'open an intercourse' with people. But part of his nature resisted. Playing with imaginary characters was much easier than responding to real ones. All his life he spoke of 'the heart' as something that needed constant attention and encouragement, needed will-power and work behind it, not to wither and dwindle away. He was, it appears, strongly tempted to dissipate reality, and especially the reality of other people and their demands on him, by absorbing himself in stories which he did not really believe; to divert all his energy to the creation of an imaginary universe which he could dismiss at will, and which could never, therefore, achieve independent reality. He found a temporary safety from this temptation in marriage; but it seems from the history of the years after his return from Europe that it renewed its attack on him and finally triumphed.

This is the picture that emerges from Newton Arvin's account of Hawthorne's life. It is of course somewhat simplified, and relies heavily on Hawthorne's own testimony; perhaps it overlooks the mitigating features. But it is much more convincing than an interpretation based on those mitigating features alone, as Mark van Doren's and Randall Stewart's seem to be.

The notebooks are full of evidence that this temptation was in fact the problem that interested Hawthorne most, and most personally; that this was the experience that demanded expression in him, which he approached, backwards, so often, and which gave that disturbing echo to his cheerfully pitched voice, in, for instance, 'Wakefield'. In 1837 he wrote:

Insincerity in a man's own heart must make all his enjoyments, all that concerns him, unreal; so that his whole life must seem like a merely dramatic representation. And this would be the case even though he were surrounded by true-hearted relatives and friends.

The precision and sombreness of his observations on this theme are far superior to anything else in the notebooks. In 1838:

Character of a man who, in himself and his external circumstances, shall be equally and totally false; his fortune resting on baseless credit—his patriotism assumed—his domestic affections, his honor and honesty, all a sham. His own misery in the midst of it—it making the whole universe, heaven and earth alike, an unsubstantial mockery to him.

Let us note that the insincerity and the falsity are not only in the man's relations with the outside world, but also in himself; so that everything is *unreal* to him. These are the thoughts, the experience, we must recall when he describes those years in such terms as 'dreamy', 'dreary', 'idle musing', 'the Dreamland of my youth', and 'an attempt to open an intercourse with the world'. In his letters to his wife he was always quite explicit about the unreality, the unsubstantiality, of his life before he met her. And if we remember the mid-Victorian standard of sensibility, sympathy, warm-heartedness (a standard his wife lived up to, and Hawthorne acted up to in his public *persona*—all the 'sweet young girls' and 'dainty little children' he invoked), then we need not wonder that this kind of guilt should have been so appalling, so unspeakable.

In his fiction, his tales and romances, this disease shows its effects most obviously in his delight in unreality. He plays on the doubtful distinction between appearance and reality, especially in the matter of the supernatural, more than any other writer. He is always pretending that something frightening or abnormal has happened (that Mistress Hibbins is literally a witch) without letting go of a safe contrasting ordinariness underneath. It appears also in his descriptions. His finest pieces of this kind, for instance that of Peterborough Close, or the gardens of the Villa Borghese, have an extraordinarily suspended, timeless, unreal quality: the exact opposite of the quality D. H. Lawrence caught in his descriptions. And in his last piece of fiction, *Septimius Felton*, we find the same painful chord being struck as in the early years.

> Septimius went into his house, and sat in his study for some hours, in that unpleasant state of feeling which a man of brooding thought is apt to experience when the world around him is in a state of intense action, which he finds it impossible to sympathize with. There seemed to be a stream rushing past him, by which, even if he plunged into the midst of it, he could not be wet. He felt himself strangely ajar with the human race, and would have given much either to be in full accord with it or to be separated from it forever.

The simplicity and vividness of the metaphor in the second sentence, and the recklessness of the last, are a guarantee that Hawthorne's imagination was excited personally by this theme.

I am dissevered from . . . the human race . . . It is my doom to
be only a spectator of life; to look on as one apart from it . . .
How cold I am now, while this whirlpool of public feeling is
eddying around me! It is as if I had not been born of woman.

III

So far, however, this reading of Hawthorne does not differ importantly from that of many critics who include him in the
highest pantheon. Newton Arvin, for instance, thinks him a sick
man but a great writer.

Hawthorne himself aimed at being a *good* writer, in the Vic-
torian sense, with a charming, cheerful, humorous style, tolerant,
bourgeois, warm-hearted, full of honest sentiment and stout common sense. He hoped his tales would pass an hour pleasantly,
cause an agreeable shudder, even dampen the eye of an especially
soft-hearted maiden; greatness he did not aim at.

This, moreover, is the Hawthorne Henry James admired. In
James's comments on the notebooks and on Hawthorne's style in
general, it is the word 'charming' that recurs more than any other.
But modern readers find Hawthorne unsuccessful in this genre.
All his children are little personages, all his girls snowy virgins,
who trip instead of walking, all his boys honest youths, all un-
married women ancient or withered or decayed maidens. Reading Hawthorne, you never touch reality, but a thick layer of
literary quilting.

In short, to bring the matter at once to a point, it was incon-
trovertibly evident that somebody had taken the shop and
fixtures of the long-retired and forgotten Mr. Pyncheon and
was about to renew the enterprise of that long-departed worthy
with a different set of customers.

A thick wadding of words interposes between the reader and the
object; and those words have in them no freshness or tension;
they come from the stock-pile of literary language.

The emotion, moreover, often strikes us as false and even un-
generous; unless we suppose his control of language so very

clumsy as to absolve him of all responsibility. The whole treatment of Hepzibah Pyncheon is an example of this. She

> began what it would be mockery to term the adornment of her
> person. Far from us be the indecorum of assisting, even in
> imagination, at a maiden lady's toilet! Our story must therefore
> await Miss Hepzibah at the threshold of her chamber; only
> presuming, meanwhile, to note some of the heavy sighs that
> laboured from her bosom, with little restraint as to their
> lugubrious depth and volume ... We suspect Miss Hepzibah,
> moreover, of taking a step upward into a chair, in order to give
> heedful regard to her appearance on all sides, and full length, in
> the oval, dingy-framed, toilet glass, that hangs above her table.
> Truly! well indeed! who would have thought it! Is all this
> precious time to be lavished on the matutinal repair and beauti-
> fying of an elderly person....

This is obviously intended to be charming, as well as graceful. In
between his exclamatory titterings, he describes her prayers and
her kissing her brother's picture quite solemnly. But no one who
reads it honestly can find it anything but offensive.

> And therefore, since we have been unfortunate enough to in-
> troduce our heroine at so inauspicious a juncture, we would
> entreat for a mood of due solemnity in the spectators of her
> fate.

Here again Hawthorne has miscalculated the readers' reactions
with a completeness that compromises his claims to be a writer at
all.

> It was overpoweringly ridiculous—we must honestly confess
> it—the deportment of the maiden lady while setting her shop
> in order for the public eye ... Our miserable old Hepzibah!
> It is a heavy annoyance to a writer, who endeavours to represent
> nature, its various attitudes and circumstances, in a reasonably
> correct outline and true colouring, that so much of the mean
> and ludicrous should be so hopelessly mixed up with the purest
> pathos which life anywhere supplies to him.

One is tempted to accuse him of hypocrisy as well as spite, since
he has gone to such lengths to make her ridiculous. But the point

c

at issue is merely that this is bad writing, so bad as to destroy, almost by itself, all claims for Hawthorne in the genre he himself most prized.

Above all, however, it is the accents of intelligence we miss in Hawthorne's editorial voice; the companionship he offers us fails worst in its vulgarity of thought. When the stories deal with science, inventions, or magic, for instance, we find a mismating of intellectual categories which seems to imply a startling lack of understanding. Take for instance 'The Artist of the Beautiful'. Owen Warland, the Artist, is a watchmaker; but he is obsessed with the Idea of the Beautiful; so he makes a mechanical butterfly; this machine responds to thought-waves; but also to moral quality in a person; and its design is the result of a deep study of butterflies. This is just the kind of grotesque muddle which, in science fiction, alienates the literate reader's confidence. In the notebooks we find 'low', 'vulgar', 'crude', 'ungentlemanly', employed as flatly and uncritically as in the worst use of the times. Key concepts like Christian and poetic are defined very genteelly. 'Today I heard a dirty mother laughing and priding herself on the pretty ways of her dirty infant—just as a Christian mother might in a nursery or drawing-room.' There can be few good writers among those who equate Christianity with cleanliness, or at least among those who could write down and preserve such a sentence. Poetry he equated with unworldliness and other-worldliness. He declared that the English could not be poetic or even intellectual because they were so rosy and thickset. 'Our pale, thin, Yankee aspect is the fitter garniture for poets.' The use of the word 'garniture' alone hinders our listening to him with attention.

IV

The most crucial instances of this imprecision in Hawthorne's mind, and also of that coldness of temperament which spoiled his geniality, occur when he treats the theme of the Unpardonable Sin. This sin Hawthorne most often specifies as Pride, and the critics have agreed with him, but here for once they have paid him too respectful attention. Ethan Brand is not proud. His wincing away from the vulgar crowd, his self-isolation in private thoughts, his self-dramatization, are evidences rather of a lack of that normal pride that keeps one robustly indifferent to the world. The two characteristics common to all Hawthorne's 'proud' heroes is that they feel themselves to be cold and indifferent to other people, and that they feel they have violated the privacy of other souls by 'using' them for their own satisfaction. In other words, they share the emotional paralysis and the narcotic dissipation of reality which Hawthorne felt himself helplessly guilty of. The word 'Pride', like the idea of an Unpardonable Sin and the stories of 'scientific' experiments, merely confuses the issue.

What Hawthorne in fact meant can be exemplified a hundredfold from his writing. Here, for instance, is a passage on John Brown.

> Nobody was ever more justly hanged. He won his martydom fairly, and took it fairly. He himself, I am persuaded, (such was his integrity), would have acknowledged that Virginia had a natural right to take the life which he had staked and lost; although it would have been better for her, in the hour that is fast coming, if she could generously have forgotten the criminality of his attempt in its enormous folly. On the other hand, any common-sensible man, looking at the matter unsentimentally, must have felt a certain intellectual satisfaction in seeing him hanged, if it were only in requital of his preposterous miscalculation of possibilities.

There is some spite against John Bown discernible there. But the real force of that last sentence is that it is unemotional; the writer is in fact taking intellectual satisfaction in seeing John Brown hanged because he miscalculated the possibilities. Put this beside the contemporary official feeling for the sacredness of a man's life, which Hawthorne endorsed in a thousand places, and the remark becomes deeply shocking. This kind of sentence often escaped Hawthorne's private censorship; about the Civil War he wrote, 'I wish they would push on the war a little more briskly. The excitement had an invigorating effect on me for a time, but it begins to lose its influence.' The sentences that did not escape his censorship, those that nobody heard but himself, presumably constituted the Unpardonable Sin.

The famous sentence about English women would not have been written by a Victorianly warm, or even a normal, sensibility. 'The grim, red-faced monsters! Surely a man would be justified in murdering them—in taking a sharp knife and cutting away their mountainous flesh until he had brought them into reasonable shape.' Or this, in a letter to his wife: 'We hold the fate of England in our hands, and it is time we crushed her—blind, ridiculous, old lump of beef, sodden in strong beer, that she is; not but what she has still vitality enough to do us a good deal of mischief, before we quite annihilate her.' Or this, about the nation as a whole: 'They feel nothing, and bring themselves no nearer to God when they pray than when they play at cards.' This is the paralysis of the heart Hawthorne spoke of, and the violation of other people's privacy. This is what made his performance as the genial author implausible, and this is the experience he was always obliquely referring to. There was no pride in this.

V

But if Hawthorne was not a good writer, perhaps he was a great one. Perhaps, on his own obsessive themes, he transcended his own intentions, and delivered a profound, tragic, truth. This is much more what the critics claim for him, and it is indeed obvious that Hawthorne had some of the qualifications for writing a very remarkable book. Let us take two examples of his most celebrated tales, and try to justify our resistance to the claims made for them.

'Young Goodman Brown' is said to be a Pilgrim's Progress in reverse, an anti-Puritan allegory. But the prose is not at all evocative of such meanings; it offers no evidence that the writer knew anything about faith or morality. 'Martha Carrier, who had received the devil's promise to be queen of hell. A rampant hag was she.' Hawthorne's language refers us immediately to the world of inferior literature. Bunyan's referred us to the world of common objects, and to a system of theology and morals fervently believed in. 'On he flew among the black pines, brandishing his staff with frenzied gestures, now giving vent to an inspiration of horrid blasphemy, and now shouting forth such laughter as set all the echoes of the forest laughing like demons around him.' Nothing there evokes the experience of blasphemy. Everything evokes memories of fanciful fiction. 'Another verse of the hymn arose, a slow and mournful strain, such as the pious love, but joined to words which expressed all that our natures can conceive of sin, and darkly hinted at far more.' This is the language of empty exaggeration; after all that our natures can conceive comes 'far more'. 'Young Goodman Brown' is not an allegory because it allegorizes nothing. There is no experience embodied in it.

'Ethan Brand' begins with a roar of laughter far off 'like wind shaking the boughs of a forest'. We hear the voice of children's ghost stories crudely superimposed on that of the clubman author. But it is the handling of the Unpardonable Sin, and the IDEA, which most chills our responsiveness. It seems to indicate that Hawthorne does not know the experience he is discussing first-hand, that he thinks about it as well as writing about it, all in capital letters. 'That portentous night when the IDEA was first developed' tells the reader that the author does not know what it is like to have such an idea. He seems to confuse a fascination with the moral problem of sin with philosophical inquiry in general, and that again with a practical experimentation in something like hypnotism or animal magnetism. Ethan Brand had been

a simple and loving man, watching his fire in the years gone by, and ever musing as it burned. . . . Then ensued that vast intellectual development, which, in its progress, disturbed the counterpoise between his mind and heart. The Idea that possessed his life had operated as a means of education; it had gone on cultivating his powers to the highest point of which they were susceptible; it had raised him from the level of an unlettered laborer to stand on a star-lit eminence, whither the philosophers of the earth, laden with lore of universities, might

vainly strive to clamber after him. So much for the intellect!
But where was the heart? That, indeed, had withered—had
contracted—had hardened—had perished! . . . he was now a
cold observer, looking on mankind as the subject of his experiment, and at length, converting man and woman to be his
puppets, and pulling the wires that moved them to such degrees
of crime as were demanded for his study.

It is not necessary to point out again the essential identity between
the character's experience and the author's, or the incongruity of
this with the story of practical experiments, and degrees of crime,
and vast intellectual development. Quite apart from that, one
cannot respond to the passage in the way the critics suggest because its ideas are handled ignorantly. There *is* no counterpoise
between the head and the heart. Preoccupation with a moral
problem does *not* give one the kind of intellectual distinction
described. The development of the intellect does *not* mean
the withering of the heart. Neither moral nor intellectual
inquiry into the nature of sin leads one into practical experiment
in crime. This is all summed up in that phrase 'vast intellectual development'; as an evocation of intellectual experience
it is like 'twenty million million diamonds' as an evocation of
wealth.

The same kind of objections apply to the other stories. 'The
Birthmark' and 'Egotism; or the Bosom-Serpent', for instance,
suffer from the same emptiness as 'Young Goodman Brown'.
The moral experience behind them is unsuccessfully integrated
into their symbolism. The notebooks are full of entries which
note, for instance, a legend about a bloody footprint, and which
end, 'This could be symbolical of something.' That is the epitaph
of all Hawthorne's symbolism. 'Wakefield', on the other hand,
could have made a wonderful book. It was exactly Hawthorne's
subject. But he didn't write it. He wrote about it instead. He
turned away from the too-direct challenge. He had to disguise
and muffle his guilt in the vague rhetoric of 'Ethan Brand'. 'O
mankind, whose brotherhood I have cast off, and trampled thy
great heart beneath my feet.'

VI

The critics' essential claim, however, is that in a few cases, above all in *The Scarlet Letter*, Hawthorne's art, working perhaps against his own intentions, delivered a profound and tragic meaning. We cannot counter those claims point by point; partly because they are so numerous and so fully developed; but mostly because we deny their starting-point. All we can do is offer some justification for that denial, for our refusal to begin to respond to the evocations of the story.

First of all, the book's claims to be historical are so insistent and so unacceptable. Hawthorne presents his seventeenth-century people as dramatically and radically unlike his readers, because of their distance in time.

> Morally, as well as materially, there was a coarser fibre in those wives and maidens of old English birth and breeding than in their fair descendants, separated from them by a series of six or seven generations; for throughout that chain of ancestry, every successive mother has transmitted to her child a fainter bloom, a more delicate and briefer beauty, and a slighter physical frame, if not a character of less force and solidity, than her own.

This is a very crude and unhistorical version of historicity (by such a system medieval man becomes neolithic) and it has the additional disadvantage of prescribing a quite barbarous use of language for these people. Thus the children of Boston are represented as saying to each other, 'Behold, verily, there is the woman of the scarlet letter: and of a truth, moreover, there is the likeness of the scarlet letter running along by her side! Come, therefore, and let us fling mud at them.' But when Hawthorne turns to his main characters he makes no attempt to make them 'seventeenth century' or historically true in any sense. T. S. Eliot has said that Hawthorne's is a true criticism of the Puritan morality, true because it has the fidelity of the artist and not a mere conviction of the man; but there is very little that is Puritan in *The Scarlet Letter*. The thoughts and emotions expressed all belong to the nineteenth century. The only one of the main characters who is even said to hold Puritan beliefs, is Dimmesdale, and he is a perfectly Rousseauish hero. He is the man of sensibility. His preaching style, his physical frailty, his pallor, his eloquent, tremulous voice, his lofty brow and hollow cheek and burning eye, all these announce the romantic hero, quite incongruously translated into seventeenth-century Boston. He is no more a study in Puritanism than is Edgar Linton in *Wuthering Heights*, and the affront to our historical sense (so insistently aroused by the writer) is one of the minor sources for our distrust of the book.

More importantly, the book is full of inconsistencies. When Dimmesdale saw the scarlet letter in the sky, Hawthorne tells us that though a nation's destiny might worthily be thought to be revealed in an astronomical portent, this could not be true for an individual. He could only think he read his own fate there if he,

> rendered morbidly self-contemplative by long, intense, and secret pain, had extended his egotism over the whole expanse of nature . . . We impute it, therefore, solely to the disease in his own eye and heart, that the minister, looking upward to the zenith, beheld there the appearance of an immense letter—the letter A—marked out in lines of dull red light.

Quite clearly, therefore, there was no such phenomenon. But next morning the sexton says: 'But did your reverence hear of the portent that was seen last night—a great letter in the sky—the letter A?' So there was such a phenomenon, visible to others. These inconsistencies are usually explained as examples of Hawthorne's irony. That point must be answered later. For the moment let us offer only the alternative explanation that Hawthorne had not noticed his mistake.

But most important of all, since the book is said to be a study of the psychology of sin, we do not believe in Hawthorne's understanding of complex characters or emotions. Let us take Chillingworth as an example, and claim that his character does not develop during the book. We are told that he changed greatly, but we are shown nothing of it; in fact we are given evidence that he did not.

We are told that when Chillingworth arrived in Boston, the

day the book opens, he was calm, just, scholarly, severe, upright in all his dealings with the world, cold but kindly. Yet his first action, when Hester sees him in the crowd, was that a writhing horror twisted itself across his face, and he signed to her not to recognize him. Neither reaction is congruous with the character he is given. Such a man, cold, selfish, just, had nothing to lose by coming forward. Such a man, with no sexual passion for his wife, had no reason for a writhing horror. One can imagine, indeed, a selfish anger with Hester, for disgracing him and disappointing him of the conjugal comforts he had hoped for; one can imagine the gradual development, within that anger, of primitive passions hitherto unawakened in him; but that is not what Hawthorne describes. What is described is of the same kind of melodramatic diabolism as his behaviour at the end of the book. We are shown no development.

We are given no reason for Chillingworth's being in the Puritan settlement at all. There is no hint of religious feeling in him, in the present or the past. A scholar, remote from all emotional or practical problems, he was surely the last type of man to leave Europe for the New World. Moreover, given his view of Hester as a beautiful object and a cheering influence, it is equally difficult to understand his sending her ahead, alone, to wait two years for him in such extraordinary circumstances. Surely the most satisfactory explanation of these oddities is that Hawthorne did not think of them; because he was not dealing in human realities but in stage properties. But even if you think he was dealing in truths of the heart, and that these truths of contingency were not immediately relevant, the fact remains that an author who offers crude implausibilities of this kind forfeits our confidence.

In the scene in prison Chillingworth is shown as (implausibly) dispassionate with Hester, but implacably bent on destroying the seducer.

'But, Hester, the man lives who has wronged us both' . . . with a smile of dark and self-relying intelligence . . . 'I shall seek this man, as I have sought truth in books; as I have sought gold in alchemy. . . . Sooner or later he must needs be mine!'

The eyes of the wrinkled scholar glowed so intensely upon
her ... 'Thine acts are like mercy,' said Hester, bewildered and
appalled, 'But thy words interpret thee as a terror ... Why dost
thou smile at me so?' inquired Hester, troubled at the expression of his eyes. 'Art thou like the Black Man that haunts the
forest round us? Hast thou enticed me into a bond that will
prove the ruin of my soul?' 'Not thy soul,' he answered, with
another smile, 'No, not thine.'

This is the first day of the action of the book, and Chillingworth
is as diabolical as he ever becomes. He is already on the track,
dark, stealthy, furious. He is already identified with the devil,
with a snake, with the Black Man. He accepts that identification
himself, in his last remark. Yet in Chapter 10 Hawthorne says,

> He had begun an investigation, as he imagined, with the severe
> and equal integrity of a judge, desirous only of truth, even
> as if the question involved no more than the air-drawn lines
> and figures of a geometrical problem, instead of human pas-
> sions, and wrongs inflicted on himself.

This is as flat a contradiction as one could find in fiction.

The next time we see Chillingworth is at the Governor's Hall,
a third of the way through the book, when he is 'much uglier—
how his dark complexion seemed to have grown duskier, and his
figure more misshapen'. (This is repeated every so often throughout the book; but one hardly calls this development.) He is walking very close beside Dimmesdale, always whispering in his ear,
and directing significant remarks at him. 'Would it be beyond a
philosopher's research, think ye, gentlemen, to analyse that child's
nature, and, from its make and mould, to give a shrewd guess at
the father?' By all the devices of fiction, that is, we are given to
understand that he knows Dimmesdale to be Hester's seducer; or
at least he suspects him and is probing his conscience. But we
have not, let us note, been shown, or even told about, the birth of
this suspicion. In a study of this kind, surely such a moment cries
out for some kind of treatment. Hawthorne merely omits it.
Nor does he, in this scene, tell us anything about the form or
function of the suspicion. He parades the two men before our

eyes, gives them a couple of perfunctory gestures, and whisks them away again.

His account of Chillingworth's probing, when it does come, is purely rhetorical.

> So Roger Chillingworth—the man of skill, the kind and friendly physician—strove to go deep into his patient's bosom, delving among his principles, prying into his recollections, and probing everything with a cautious touch, like a treasure-seeker in a dark cavern.

This is a picture of the idea of the thing; a reader might talk like that, describing Porfiry Petrovitch's conversations with Raskolnikov. Dostoevski, however, did not talk like that; he gave us the reality.

Then, at this point in the book, it is insinuated—as a device of fiction it amounts to an assertion—that Chillingworth had been mixed up in the Overbury murder case, was a friend of Dr. Forman's, and that he had joined in evil Indian rituals. If this is true, it makes nonsense of the purity, justice, and uprightness he was credited with on arrival. If it is not true, what is it there for?

Then comes the crucial scene in which he uncovers Arthur's chest, and sees whatever he sees there, and throws his arms up and stamps on the floor and exults like the devil. We gather that he discovered something important then.

> After the incident last described, the intercourse between the clergyman and the physician, though externally the same, was really of another character than it had previously been. The intellect of Roger Chillingworth had now a sufficiently plain path before it. . . . Calm, gentle, passionless as he appeared, there was yet, we fear, a quiet depth of malice, hitherto latent, but active now, in this unfortunate old man.

In what sense the malice had been latent before is difficult to discover. As far as the reader is concerned (and the author is presumably addressing the reader) he has never appeared calm, gentle, or passionless; and the other characters, we have been told, instinctively felt him to be diabolical.

A revelation, he could almost say, had been granted to him. It mattered little, for his object, whether celestial, or from what other region. By its aid, in all the subsequent relations betwixt him and Mr. Dimmesdale, not merely the external presence, but the very inmost soul, of the latter, seemed to be brought out before his eyes, so that he could see and comprehend its every movement.... He could play upon him as he chose.

But what had been discovered? That Arthur had been Hester's lover? He knew that before. That Arthur was suffering? He knew that. That there was a red A on Arthur's chest? This, as something extra to its meanings, which he was already sure of, could not *tell* him very much. Of course, it would be a gratification; one understands the dance of joy; but what information was conveyed, what clue given, what path was *now* opened before Chillingworth's intellect?

There is no development in the book. We are told, many times, that Chillingworth came to Boston calm and studious, and became dark and devilish. But we are not shown how this happened. We get no insight into the process. We are told that he long suspected and finally discovered that Dimmesdale was Hester's seducer; but we get no insight into the process of suspicion. We are told that he tortured his victim; but we do not see this happen. What we do see is a fundamental confusion in Hawthorne's mind about the characters and incidents of his fable. We have therefore no readiness to respond to any of the book's dramatic moments, no readiness to believe the critics when they construct large interpretations of them.

VII

Hawthorne himself rated *The Scarlet Letter* below *The House of the Seven Gables*; just as he 'could not remember' what his 'blasted allegories' were about. For him *The Scarlet Letter* was a 'gloomy' book, and he preferred his sunnier work. A plain reading must surely lead one to agree with him. However, there is no hope of convincing, with one short article, those who have invested thought and emotion in an opposite valuation, or of answering all

the multifold objections that must spring to their lips. But one
point can be tackled. Hawthorne's most complete inconsistencies
are usually dismissed by claiming that they are example of his
irony; that he meant to keep us in doubt, for instance, about
whether there was a scarlet letter in the sky. Hawthorne is taken
to be the most ironical writer of the nineteenth century; the only
member of the New England Renaissance too subtle to be satisfied with Emerson's facile optimism.

It is indeed obvious that it was Hawthorne's general policy to
avoid committing himself on every issue, and to take up more
than one attitude to it. But whether in any particular case this
deserves the name of irony, must depend on whether there is any
point made by the equivocation, and any evidence that the writer
took responsibility finally for one of the alternatives. If not, it
remains an equivocation, or, in instances like this of the letter in
the sky, a mistake. For Hawthorne certainly was not asking us to
believe that an astronomical portent actually occurred. That
would be against his insistent practice of providing a possible
natural explanation for every supernatural appearance. This
time he forgot his escape route.

It is our case that there is no *a priori* reason to accept *any*
ambiguity in Hawthorne as meaningful irony: that it is usually a
device of caution or a carelessness. In support of that, we can
point to ample evidence, in the prose, the characterization, the
narrative, that Hawthorne did occasionally make mistakes, and
did habitually equivocate. We can also point to evidence of
habitual *navïeté*.

When an uninstructed multitude attempts to see with its eyes, it
is exceedingly apt to be deceived. When, however, it forms its
judgements, as it usually does, on the intuitions of its great
and warm heart, the conclusions thus attained are often so profound and so unerring, as to possess the character of truths
supernaturally revealed.

If a man were capable of useful irony, the sort that is a finer wisdom
then Emerson's, it would prevent his saying that. Then Hawthorne compares Hester on the scaffold to a Madonna and child,

and continues: 'Here there was the taint of deepest sin in the most sacred quality of human life, working such effect that the world was only the darker for this woman's beauty, and the more lost for the infant that she had borne.' This is explicit and extreme. At other times, however, he takes the opposite attitude: 'What we did had a consecration of its own.' If this inconsistency is ironical, what is the point of the irony, and which was Hawthorne's final position? The question is unanswerable. These are, in fact, recognizably the two halves of the stock Victorian-fiction attitude to the fallen woman; public condemnation and private reverence; the incompatibility of the two in Hawthorne is due to greater *naïveté*, not irony.

Hawthorne's availability for the defence of irony is no accident. It is partly because of his habit of equivocation that he has been included in the modern pantheon of American literature, partly because of his rejection of realism. For the last thirty years or more, all the brightest minds in American criticism have been guided by an enthusiasm for irony and symbolism in art, for tragedy, history, a sense of evil, as the materials of art; and an aversion from the self-consciously noble and expansive, the uplifting, simplifying, energizing. We have had nearly half a century of anti-Emersonianism, and Hawthorne's reputation is one of its by-products.

Henry James's Subjective Adventurer: 'The Sacred Fount'

TONY TANNER

'BUT if nothing was more impossible than the fact, nothing was more intense than the vision.' These words from *In the Cage* succinctly point to a profound problem to which James addressed himself in some of his later fiction—the problem of the relationship between vision and fact. The heroine of the story is a poor telegraphist whose position is, for James, a very suggestive one. She works at the very hub of society, reading clues, deciphering hints, thriving on suggestions, and at the same time she is for ever excluded from an active recognized part in that society. Her dreams, her theories, her ever-expanding speculations are her compensation, even her vocation: they are made possible by her curious situation of being at once intimate with and alienated from the arcana of high society. For her the opportunity to see and speculate constitutes a privilege more valuable than her own humdrum life spent with her fiancé, the lower-class Mr. Mudge. The essential difference between her and Mr. Mudge—her essential rarity—is brought out in a passage concerning their visit to Bournemouth. They both visit the band-stand, the noisy centre of the town life, but their appetites and interests differ.

> She preferred to sit at the far end, away from the band and the crowd; as to which she had frequent differences with her friend, who reminded her often that they could have only in the thick of it the sense of the money they were getting back. That had little effect on her, for she got back her money by seeing many things, the things of the past year, fall together and connect themselves, undergo the happy relegation that transforms

melancholy and misery, passion and effort, into experience and knowledge.

Mr. Mudge leads a purely physical existence—he voices the claims of the creature who wishes to join the herd. The heroine prefers to remain away from it all—considering her money well spent if she can be left to her work of imaginative reconstruction, allowing the mind to find order and connection where it will, endowing the arbitrary with a sense of sequence, redeeming life from chaos, making facts serve the need of vision.

In the Cage is minor—but important. For here in miniature James has submitted the habit of speculation to a comic exaggeration and at the same time asserted its purpose and value. As a person the telegraphist must go away with Mr. Mudge to Chalk Farm—but as a principle she represents for James the function and predicament of the artist. The price she has to pay is exclusion from participation—indeed it is the very condition of her work: the profit is, however, large—the imaginative transformation of the world. The action of the story is, wrote James, 'simply the girl's "subjective" adventure': she is one of those few people for whom consciousness in itself is 'a romance', one of those rare and privileged people who are gifted with 'the critical impulse and the acuter vision'. James became increasingly interested in what he equivocally called 'the morbid imagination', 'that rash, that idle faculty [which] continues to abound in questions, and to supply answers to as many of them as possible'—and his most profound examination of this faculty is *The Sacred Fount*, written in 1901 just before he embarked on his last major phase.

The theme of the book is not so esoteric as some critics have made out: it fits in with one of James's recurring preoccupations. Briefly: the narrator tells of a week-end visit to a country house called Newmarch. On the train going down he notes that a man—Gilbert Long—whom he once considered dull and stupid, now seems bright and intelligent. He also notes that a lady—Grace Brissenden—whom he knows to be old, seems in fact to be growing younger and more vivacious with the years. On later meeting her husband—Briss—he fancies him to be old and exhausted. On the strength of these impressions the narrator starts to construct a theory—a theory which is at first helped by equivocal hints from other people. The theory is based on the idea of the depletion and appropriation of human energy—particularly between the sexes. The 'sacred fount' of the life force is 'like the greedy man's description of the turkey as an "awkward" dinner dish. It may be sometimes too much for a single share, but it's not enough to go round.' Thus in any marriage one person will be a taker, the other a giver. '"One of the pair," I said, "has to pay for the other".' A conversation with Mrs. Brissenden brings this out more clearly. She speaks first:

'One of them always gets more out of it than the other. One of them—you know the saying—gives the lips, the other gives the cheek.'

'It's the deepest of all truths. Yet the cheek profits too,' I more prudently argued.

'It profits most. It takes and keeps and uses all the lips give.'

Is is those characters in James who 'take and keep and use' the sacred life energy of another person who are the real villains—whether one cares to think of Olive Chancellor trying to draw Verena Tarrant into her freezing orbit, or Gilbert Osmond exploiting Isabel Archer for his sterile ends, or the more minor cruelty exercised by Lady Beldonald in *The Beldonald Holbein* or the 'atrocity of art' with which Mrs. Grantham takes her revenge on the innocent Lady Gwyther in *The Two Faces*, the general fault common to all is that they batten on other people, use them, manipulate them, exploit them, make them over for their own ends, instead of reverencing their unique and independent jet of life. The narrator's theory, then, is related to a central Jamesian concern, and in the light of this theory he is sure that just as Briss seems to be 'paying' for his wife, so some lady must be paying for the unbelievably enhanced and energized Gilbert Long. His improvement is such that she must be paying a great deal—she must be almost drained of her own spirit and wit. So he sets about looking for 'the right idiot'—right, that is, for his

theory. One could almost put it this way—he is trying to find
warrant for writing a James novel.

Newmarch is no ordinary country house. It is 'a place of charm
so special as to create rather a bond among its guests'. It is sometimes discussed in theatrical terms—'an ample stage'—and it is
clearly more emblematic than real: 'life became a mere arrested
ramble or stimulated lounge, and we profited to the full by the
noble freedom of Newmarch, that over-arching ease which in
nothing was so marked as in the tolerance of talk. The air of the
place itself, in such conditions, left one's powers with a sense of
play; if one wanted something to play at one simply played at
being there.' It is a sort of ideal world in which people are released from all material contingencies and provided with a
setting which most encourages and permits them to indulge their
talent for forming relationships. 'Was *any* temporary collocation,
in a house so encouraging to sociability, out of the range of
nature?' It has all the appearance of being James's version of
paradise, a sort of Platonic idea of 'society'. Certainly all the chal-
lenges which James found in society are here in an extreme form.
The atmosphere of the house is one of 'clear dimness and rich
gleams' and in this ambiguous brilliant dusk the relationship between appearances and reality is almost preternaturally difficult to
infer and establish. Every room leads to another room—there
are 'great chains' of rooms—and everybody seems a possible
screen for somebody else until the whole place seems to be composed of nothing but screens, and every spoken thing seems a
mask for an unspoken gesture of sinister portent. The consensus
of gracious forms at some times seems to be an expression of mankind's finest social instincts; and at other times it seems a pro-
longed massive charade of non-expressive and concealing postures.
At times the atmosphere of the house is distinctly oppressive, as
when the narrator walks out into the garden and finds the air 'a
sudden corrective to the grossness of our lustres and the thickness
of our medium, our general heavy humanity'. More remarkable
is the narrator's meditation in the garden. 'We were all so fine
and formal, and the ladies in particular at once so little and so
much clothed, so beflounced yet so denuded, that the summer

stars called to us in vain. We had ignored them in our crystal cage, among our tinkling lamps; no more free really to alight than if we had been dashing in a locked railway-train across a lovely land.' That society might be abysmal, that it might be a condemnation and a sentence, a suffocating and weary imprisonment, that there might be terror as well as beauty in 'conditions so highly organized'—these pessimistic feelings are part of the late James's ambivalent attitude towards society. Newmarch is the social world, and the narrator goes back into it to continue his quest: but while, as a house, it is not so horrifying as Atreus's palace in *Agamemnon*, or the guilt-saturated mansion of *Rosmersholm*, it is a place more of darkness than light and there is a hint of something mephitic in the thick social air.

In its populated gloom the one thing necessary is some guiding light, and since society has come to ignore the stars and preferred the inadequate substitute of its 'tinkling lamps' the narrator's quest is really for some sort of better illumination—in every sense of that word. When he speaks of 'raking the gloom for lights' he reveals himself in his most suggestive stance. All his ideas and fancies are spoken of in terms of light: 'a blaze of suggestion', 'the flame of my fancy', 'sparks were what we wanted' and so on. His theory acts as 'a torch in the darkness': as he says— 'I start, for my part, at any rate, quite in the dark—or in a darkness—lighted, at best, by what you have called the torch of my analogy.' In this book, as in many others by James, the importance of eyesight is stressed continually. From the start the narrator 'watches with curiosity', he is always attracted by the prospect of there being 'something for me to see'. He always wants 'a glimpse'—a word to which he often recurs and which, as with the girl in the cage, seems to indicate a preferred mode of seeing. For glimpses stimulate the imagination as a revealed panorama seen in absolute clarity would not. Typically he refers to the 'general, amiable consensus of blindness' around him in such a way as to dignify and sanctify his dedication to the holy task of 'the very act of seeing'. He likes to 'watch and watch' and lives in a separate 'world of observation' to such an extent that he attracts the accusation—'You see too much'. His defence is that

'one couldn't know anything without seeing all'—but in this
case 'seeing', unlike the faculty exercised by early Jamesian pro-
tagonists, but like that of the girl in the cage, is a source of
visions. 'Observation breeds ideas' as he puts it, and he elsewhere
talks of 'the momentum already acquired by the act of observation'. His 'extraordinary interest in my fellow-creatures' stimu-
lates his eyes, and seen glimpses promote imagined speculations.
And speculation—this is the main point—is a source of illumination.

It is also important to note that speculation is also allied to
'creation'. 'To see all this was at the time, I remember, to be
inhumanly amused as if one had found one could create something. I had created nothing but a clue or two to the larger com-
prehension I still needed, yet I positively found myself overtaken
by a mild artistic glow.' More than that, at one crucial point the
lady Mrs. Server, whom he suspects to be his missing character
and with whom he is possibly infatuated, seems to appear at the
dictates of his imagination. 'It was exactly as if she had been
there by the operation of my intelligence. . . .' At the time of this
meeting Newmarch has become like some 'castle of enchantment,
and the narrator is reminded of the 'days of fairy-tales and of the
childish imagination of the impossible'. 'In those days,' he goes on
'I moved in a world in which the strange "came true".' By extension he feels there is now a touch of 'wizardry' in his own
imaginative version of the world. 'I had thought it all out, and to
have thought it was, wonderfully, to have brought it.' Thus
when Mrs. Server finally appears in 'the thin suffusion of twilight'
there is something vaguely hallucinatory and conjured about her
presence. We feel that this encounter might be an overspill from
the 'wealth' of his imagination into the world of fact. That the
imagination might be capable of evoking its own necessary
mirages is an aspect of the book to be remembered.

But at this point we should more clearly establish what is the
motivating force behind the narrator's strenuous activity—what
drives him to his compulsive watching, his endless envisioning?
What does he mean when he speaks of being 'on the scent of something ultimate'? A key statement occurs early in the book.

I was just conscious, vaguely, of being on the track of a law, a law that would fit, that would strike me as governing the delicate phenomena—delicate though so marked—that my imagination found itself playing with. A part of the amusement they yielded came, I dare say, from my exaggerating them— grouping them into a larger mystery (and thereby a larger 'law') than the facts, as observed, yet warranted; but that is the common fault of minds for which the vision of life is an obsession.

He talks about wanting 'absolute certainty' and claims a right 'to judge of what other people did'. He also refers to 'the sense of a discovery to be made' and his 'sense of reality'—and we may be sure that he means the reality that lies muffled and obliterated under the thick pile of appearances. He wants to get at the underlying pattern, to tease out deeper meanings. He claims that 'the more things I fitted together the larger sense, every way, they made'—for him only those things which cohere can signify; the random, the contingent, the unrelated cannot yield up a meaning. It is in making things 'hook up', in finding a theory which will embrace the glimpsed facts, that he finds 'the joy of the intellectual mastery of things unamenable, that joy of determining, almost of creating results'. Like the girl in the cage he represents an activity rather than an involved character. 'I alone was magnificently and absurdly aware—everyone else was benightedly out of it.' He is one of the privileged and perhaps cursed few who care to be conscious, who seek for the higher awareness, who catechize and interrogate the surfaces of the world in an effort to find a core of meaning.

Yet though he is after an explaining law, he is also desirous of constructing a picture. That is to say he also wants to *add* something to the world—in particular those symmetries and harmonies which are alien to its gratuitous configurations. 'Things in the real had a way of not balancing; it was all an affair, this fine symmetry, of artificial proportion.' The desire to account for things leads on to the instinct to alter them or add to them in the interests of an ideal of 'composition'. The narrator continually discusses his ambition in the terms of painting and he explicitly compares his chosen task to that of the painter Obert: 'I only talk as you paint.' He talks of 'fresh accession' enriching 'the picture' and often alludes to 'my gallery'. He views chance collocations with a painter's eye and at moments his desire for composition supersedes his need for elucidation. So, referring back to his avowed search for a law, we see that he wants to establish *both* the laws which explain actual human events, *and* the laws which govern the act of artistic creation. The idea which relates these two sets of laws is that of 'analogy': the ideally composed artistic world can shed illuminating light on the fractured imperfect physical world. 'Our world is brazen: the poet only delivers a golden'. Thus Sir Philip Sidney, and without exploring the neo-platonic implications we can see that James is continuing a long aesthetic debate, the question of the relationship between the brazen and golden worlds, between vision and fact.

The narrator certainly epitomizes the artistic instinct for James. The initial line of his inquiry—is Gilbert Long having an affair which is in some way nourishing him with unexpected energy at the expense of some unknown suffering woman?—extends to the whole question of discerning or imposing a principle of order in or on the world. He talks about his theory very much as many critics have talked about a work of art; 'that special beauty of my scheme through which the whole depended so on each part and each part guaranteed the whole.' He wants and works to elicit a golden world from the brazen world—not however a world where people are better than in our world but a world in which their lives have more logic and shape. And as he talks about his golden world he continually implies that it is fragile, insubstantial, but precious. He refers to his constructed theory, his composed picture, as 'a great glittering crystal palace', 'a palace of thought', 'the kingdom of thought I had won'—though Mrs. Brissenden who most nearly understands him and most grievously threatens him refers to his speculations as 'houses of cards'. He makes his 'flight into luminous ether' and in those rarefied territories of the imagination he constructs a delicate artefact which orders and ordains the lower empiric world. But the risk is great. Having made his brilliant construction he concedes—'but there was no objective test to which I had yet exposed my theory.' Random scraps of information and alternative points of view continually threaten his 'whole airy structure'. He is often made to 'tremble for the impunity of my creation' and he comes to object to the possibility of verifying his vision. He does not wish 'to expose to the world, to defend against the world, to share with the world, that now so complex tangle of hypotheses that I have had for convenience to speak of as my theory.' He is in the position of the alienated artist, cherishing his product, and nervously guarding it against what Yeats called 'the brutality, the ill-breeding, the barbarism of truth.' (And Yeats himself constructed 'A Vision' as 'a last act of defence against the chaos of the world.') His highly organized vision becomes self-sealing and so far from explaining the life around him it becomes a consolation to be set over against that life, a preferable extension of creation. If the facts do not fit the theory—why, so much the worse for the facts. That at least is the feeling.

The relation of the narrator's art to reality is, then, a curious one. He starts his theory from a 'recognized fact'—the change in Gilbert Long—but from then on facts seem to become more of a menace and less to be desired. He says quite early to Ford Obert: 'If I had a material clue I should feel ashamed : the fact would be a deterrent.' The 'affluence' of his vision is based on 'amazingly little evidence.' In fact the less of one seems to mean more of the other. 'It would have been almost as embarrassing to have to tell them how little experience I had had in fact as to have had to tell them how much I had had in fancy.' This clearly relates him to the girl in the cage. One 'straw' picked up from the world of facts yields him a rich harvest of imagined 'possibilities.' And in the interests of his theory he sometimes reads what does not happen into the actual, and sometimes misses things which actually happen. When a recalcitrant indigestible fact seems imminent it induces intense nervousness in the narrator. 'Things *had*, from step to step, to hang together '—that is the ambition, the need : but at crucial moments they seem, worryingly enough, 'to hang a little apart.' The slightest hint can set his fantastic imagination to work—the swish of a skirt, the stoop of a back—for to him the world is seething with *suggestiveness*: but the crisis comes when he is confronted with a *fact* which not only cannot be assimilated and dissolved in the 'solution' of his theory, but which also threatens to demolish his imaginative superstructure. This is what happens at the end. His whole theory has come to depend on Mrs. Server's being the poor woman who is 'paying' for Long: but Mrs. Brissenden comes to assure him that Long is in fact having an affair with Lady John, a talkative, energetic, self-possessed woman who will not fit the requirements of his theory at all. There is something hard, ruthless and dominating about Mrs. Brissenden and she is referred to in terms of brass—and it is her brass which shatters the pure crystal of his theory. Her harsh assurance as to the *facts* leaves his vision completely dismantled—'a pile of ruins'. It is possible that she is lying, or working for her own ends; but her very presence, and what she comes to stand for, are inimical to his careful 'embroidery' work, his artistic instinct, his search for a hidden logic. For she embraces a random, unpredictable world: she disdains his imaginative efforts to describe and prescribe for the real world. 'Things are not . . . gouged out to *your* tune.' If his theory fails, his vision vanishes, and art, as it were, loses out to life.

In this book James has subjected the activities of the 'morbid imagination' to their most damaging criticisms. He allows certain key questions to be raised concerning the narrator's habit of speculation. Is this activity necessary, is it pernicious? Should he stop, can he stop? Is he neurotic, even mad? Is he so obsessed with Mrs. Server that he sees the world in a distorted manner? These are the sort of questions which James allows to be raised around the narrator. He himself sometimes feels that his curiosity is 'wanting in taste' and at certain contented moments at Newmarch he feels that there is no 'application' for 'a transcendent intelligence' and that 'we existed . . . to be really what we looked'. At other moments his 'estimate of the value of perception' undergoes a sudden reversal. He suddenly 'wished to unthink every thought with which I had been occupied for twenty-four hours'. Certainly he thinks it a bad thing to communicate his visions to other people, for that would make them 'begin to vibrate, to crack and split, from within'. If imagination and speculation are a curse, then it is one which he feels he must bear alone. More than once he proclaims his readiness to 'give up everything' and at times he envies in other people 'the state of exemption from intense obsessions' and desires to 'break off sharp' from his own. But he cannot remain detached and indifferent, he cannot make himself impervious to suggestion. His imaginative speculation seems to work autonomously, independent of his social-physical presence.

The comments of other characters add to our ambivalent assessment of the narrator. Gilbert Long says he has got Briss 'on the brain' and will not join him in his speculations. The artist Obert after following him for a while drops out—'It isn't any of one's business, is it?' Lady John accuses him of having 'the imagination of atrocity', of trying to be a 'providence' and she adds her witty warning: 'You can't be a providence and not be a bore.' Many complain of his constant questioning and his habit of trying to involve them in his meditative speculations, but it is Mrs. Brissenden who voices the most damning sequence of charges. 'You see too much'—'You talk too much'—'You're abused by a fine fancy'—'I think you're crazy.' Obviously she is his fiercest opponent, she and all she stands for, but since the narrator himself refers to his 'private madness' James clearly intends to allow the idea of the abnormality if not the insanity of art to lie like a vein through the novel. It is—we might say—the verdict of the practical world, the people who make themselves at home amongst the surface facts.

Does he inquire too curiously? 'The state of my conscience was that I knew too much—that no one had really any business to know what I knew.' But what kind of knowledge is it that disdains facts and winces at proferred information? We may call it imaginative penetration, the attempt to ensnare the essence by speculation, the registering of nuances and possibilities and suggestions which afford faint intimations of a profounder level of reality. But of course all this labour might be misdirected. It might have its origins in inward disorder, the unhealthy hypertrophy of the speculative faculty: it might spring from unacknowledged passions gone sour. It can interfere with fruitful living in the empirical world—'the lap of the actual'—and it might constitute a menace, an intrusion for less 'conscious' people. It might lead to a valuation of art over life, or an impotent solipsism. It might take a man out of the world in a number of ways. These are some of the risks for the subjective adventurer—what are the gains? Are we to dismiss the narrator as 'crazy' along with Mrs. Brissenden, or does James make him stand for a set of attitudes and activities that he valued, valued despite the attendant risks? Valued, perhaps, because those very risks make the activity heroic?

If 'art is our flounderings shown' as Colonel Voyt suggests in *The Story in it*, then the narrator's attempt to chart the tangled relations of the people around him has at least the value of drawing up a tentative map for a troubled sea. Even if the flounderings are due to the ineradicable predatory instincts of men and women—still it is better to have a pattern of pursuit and carnage than no pattern at all. Any light is at least a minor triumph against the darkness. But as the narrator comes to realize, 'the condition of light . . . was the sacrifice of feeling'. Exclusion from participation—and this relates him to other Jamesian characters, such as Strether—is 'the price of the secret success, the lonely liberty and the intellectual joy'. It is what his 'priceless pearl of an inquiry' costs—to save it he is willing to 'harden my heart'. Pearl and crystal in preference to—a live woman? We are at least allowed the hint and should take away with us some sense of the price the narrator talks about. But if his willingness to pay the price is not simply obsessional, then his sense of necessary exclusion must be due to an awareness of some higher allegiance, some more exacting responsibility. His 'providential supervision' of the social world—even if it only goes on in his head—does have a value and is a real responsibility. For in some way he is the one who strives to see among the blind, the upholder of consciousness among the unconscious.

Excluded from the frame of society, he is its artist: denied its physical embraces, he is its conscience. He is what Conrad said James himself was: 'the preserver, the keeper, the expounder of human experience.' That is why his 'curiosity matters'. Not only because it is the only way he can appease his inner drives—'the satisfaction of my curiosity is the pacification of my mind'—but also because even among the wreck of his theory he can salvage his 'understanding'. And this is an important passage. 'I couldn't save Mrs. Server, and I couldn't save poor Briss; I *could*, however, guard, to the last grain of gold, my precious sense of their loss, their disintegration and their doom.' Curiosity leads to understanding—and only understanding can develop a sense of values. The narrator is not, after all, a nosey-parker—rather he is the person whose heightened awareness and delicate sensibility introduce into the callous indifference of unconscious life a sense of good things spoiled and cruelties perpetrated, of fine things destroyed and horrors achieved. He is accused in the book of not only seeing 'horrors' but of liking them, and it is possible to see some of his curiosity as illicit, almost prurient: but his own answer is that before condemning them he likes to 'look them first well in the face'. But if 'knowing', whether through inference or in imagination, is his vocation, then a proper distribution of pity is closely involved with it. The speculation might not be for the sake of sympathy, but there is sympathy in the speculator and in the very manner of the speculation. And this idea that there might be different ways of looking at the world, different kinds of curiosity, different modes of speculation, even different kinds of knowledge, brings us to what I think is one of the most important tenets in James's work.

There is a moment early in the book when the narrator persuades Mrs. Brissenden to share his theory about the hidden source of Long's improvement. But as he listens to *her* speculating he suddenly has a sense of the cruelty in her being so 'keen' to indict Mrs. Server. Perhaps in this he is only seeing his own fault writ large, perhaps he is emotionally involved with Mrs. Server, or perhaps he is realizing that there are at least two different kinds of 'attention' that one can pay the world. He defends observation, speculation, reflection—but he is shocked at the gleam of cruelty in Mrs. Brissenden's manner of mentally pouncing on victims and fools. She lacks the artistic, the sympathetic motive.

To emphasize these two different ways of looking at the world, I would refer back to the relatively simple story *The Patagonia*. There is also a narrator to that story, and he tells of an ocean crossing made in the company of Mrs. Nettlepoint, her son Jasper, and a rather lonely girl called Grace Mavis who is crossing with them in order to marry her fiancé in France. The narrator is also an observer, and there is something in his character that 'makes me, in any situation, just inordinately and submissively *see* things'. In the curious atmosphere of the boat—detached from land entanglements as Newmarch is detached from the material limitations and impositions of day-to-day city existence—his speculations take on an almost creative resonance. The ship becomes a stage:

> The clean boards of the deck turn to the stage of a play that amuses, the personal drama of the voyage, the movement and interaction, in the strong sea-light, of figures that end by representing something—something moreover of which the interest is never, even in its keenness, too great to suffer you to slumber. I at any rate dozed to excess, stretched on my rug with a French novel, and when I opened my eyes I generally saw Jasper Nettlepoint pass with the young woman confided to his mother's care on his arm. Somehow at these moments, between sleeping and waking, I consequently felt that my French novel had set them in motion.

Yet in this dreamy proto-fictional world on which the narrator finds it so interesting to 'exercise' his mind, a real event of palpable physical tragedy is germinating. For Grace Mavis is obviously falling in love with Jasper—a selfish young man who is sporting with her to pass the time—and as obviously dreads her impending marriage. The narrator, sympathetic through his very speculations about her state of mind, takes it upon himself to issue some advice and admonishment to Jasper, who is offended but then leaves the girl alone. Very alone. 'There was an odd pang in seeing her move about alone; I felt somehow responsible for it and asked myself why I couldn't have kept my hands off.' Is he an interfering busy-body, or does he act from insight, pity and imagination? I think we are made to feel more of the latter.

Certainly when the dream is over reality intrudes in the ugliest way. The narrator says to Grace shortly before the ship docks: 'The first sight of land, at sea, changes everything ... It always affects me as waking up from a dream. It's a return to reality.' The dream-like French romance gives way to a tragic suicide—for Grace Mavis jumps from the ship at night.

It is such events, such unpleasant cruel twists to existence that James alluded to in his famous phrase—'the Medusa face of life'. These are things which art is helpless to prevent and unable fully to explain: it can only console by recording the loss and lamenting the waste. That is the narrator's function. His type of observation and curiosity in one sense do a great service to life: they provide that sort of sympathetic generosity of appreciation and the 'dignity of judgement' without which life remains an unreclaimed and unrecorded mess. But there is another kind of observation at work on the boat. The loathsome Mrs. Peck who is the busy-body supreme, hungry for derogatory tit-bits, quick to spread damning rumours, always keen to spot out something to castigate in public with malicious glee: she also pays attention, is an observer, and perhaps a 'creator' of sorts since her vicious gossip may have driven the lonely Grace Mavis to suicide. The narrator's benevolent meditative speculation bestows a benediction on life—he endows it with significance and invests it with an inner emotional logic where the surface shows only a squandering chaos. He may perhaps be mocked a little because he is 'so full of signification' but at least, as he himself protests, 'I had taken no such ferocious ... note as Mrs. Peck.' In contrast to his artistic speculations there is a ferocity of attention which mars what it touches, which destroys what it regards. This sort of attention has a withering effect—it takes life away.

In summing up the virtues which these narrators—and the artist in general—represented for James, I would pick on Natalia Haldin's compliment to the old western language teacher in *Under Western Eyes*: 'There is a way of looking on which is valuable.' And if Conrad seems too different a writer to compare with James, I would point to some of Conrad's statements which seem to corroborate the Jamesian idea of the artist. Thus in *A Personal*

Record where he defends himself against the charge of 'resignation' : 'But resignation is not indifference . . . I would fain claim for myself the faculty of so much insight as can be expressed in a voice of sympathy and compassion.' He returns to the point. 'Resignation, not mystic, not detached, but resignation open-eyed, conscious, and informed by love, is the only one of our feelings for which it is impossible to become a sham.' The Jamesian narrator could not remain detached to the point of in-difference, and it is certainly intimated that love and pity were the cause of this inability. More, he too insists on looking at horrors 'open-eyed' and he too upholds the claims of consciousness. The narrator, or perhaps we should now simply say James himself, could claim, as Conrad does, that his art has its origins in 'a senti-ment akin to piety'. For James, like Conrad, was one of those few men who, to use Conrad's fine phrase, 'know how to look at their kind'.

Obviously some basic aesthetic problems have been raised here : what is the way the artist looks at the world, does it differ from other modes of visual appropriation of the phenomenological universe, what is the relation between the artist's vision of form and the form-evading empirical data which endlessly claim his attention? I suggest that we see James's parable of the artist against the larger philosophical background. We could begin by considering Shaftesbury's opposition to empiricism.[1] Against the Baconian ideal of *scientia propter potentiam*—knowledge for the sake of power—he set up an ideal of *amor non mercenarius*—non-mercenary love. The beauty of an object is only really felt, Shaftesbury maintained, when all thoughts of possessing, en-joying, or controlling it are absent. Devotion not dominion, meditation not mastery, contemplation not conquest—these are his preferred attitudes. Thus he maintains that 'The Bridegroom-Doge' 'who in his stately *Bucentaur* floats on the Bosom of his THETIS, has less *possession* than the poor *Shepherd*, who from a

---

[1] The following passages from Shaftesbury (*Characteristics of Men and Man-ners,* 1711, incorporating *The Moralist,* 1709, and *Soliloquy,* 1710) are quoted in Ernest Cassirer's *The Platonic Renaissance in England.*

hanging Rock, or Point of some high Promontory, stretch'd at his ease, forgets his feeding Flocks, while he admires *her Beauty*'.

Admiration not appetite is the true manner of 'possessing' the beauty of the world: this is almost exactly James's own position. It is at least partially for this reason that Strether refuses participation in the European arena of the senses—he prefers to wonder at it in his own non-interfering manner. Appreciation as opposed to appropriation. For the neo-platonists—such as Shaftesbury was and James might have been—it was the part of animals to act according to the 'provoked senses', it was the high vocation of man to transcend his appetites and relish the formal principles at work in the universe. '*The Beautiful, the Fair, the Comely,* were never in the *Matter* but in the *Art* and *Design,* never in the *Body,* itself, but in the *Form* or *Forming Power.*'

Shaftesbury's concept of 'disinterested pleasure' has a profound influence on all the later German aestheticians and thus back to Coleridge, Emerson and New England culture in general. But here I would point out that the Shaftesburian artist does not interfere with the seen world, nor does he merely celebrate the surfaces of material things. By appreciating the hidden forming powers at work in the universe he is able to perceive and produce forms where the ordinary man might see only random matter open to legislation and exploitation. Because of his superior insight the artist is not bound by the gratuitous configurations of the empirical world. But to get at the difference between the matter of the world and the matter of art I would turn briefly to a modern aesthetician—Henri Focillon: and during the following quotations[1] I suggest that the narrator of *The Sacred Fount* be kept in mind.

> There is consequently between the matters or substances of art and the substances of nature a divorce, even when they are bound together by the strictest formal propriety. A new order is established, within which there are two distinct realms. . . . The wood of the statue is no longer the wood of the tree; sculptured marble is no longer the marble of the quarry; melted and hammered gold becomes an altogether new and

[1] From *La vie des formes en art.*

different metal; bricks that have been baked and then built into a wall bear no relation to the clay of the clay-pit. The colour, the integument, all the values that affect the sight have changed. Things without a surface, whether once hidden in the bark, buried in the mountain, imprisoned in the nugget, or swallowed in the mud, have become wholly separated from chaos. They have acquired an integument; they adhere to space; they welcome a daylight that works freely upon them.

It is perhaps the aim of all artists to 'separate things from chaos' and we could say that the intention of the narrator of *The Sacred Fount* is to take his raw material from the social world and re-form it into a more orderly dispensation. Focillon further maintains that 'the life of forms is never at a loss to create any matter, any substance whatsoever of which it stands in need'. He insists that it is the normal ambition of man's mind to give form to what it sees and he then defines the artist's difference from ordinary man: 'the artist develops, under our eyes, the very technique of the mind; he gives us a kind of mould or cast which we can both see and touch. But this high privilege is not merely that of being an accurate and skilful moulder of casts. He is not manufacturing a collection of solids for some psychological laboratory; he is creating a world—a world that is complex, coherent, and concrete.' The artist is not restricted to observed phenomena: he can create what the exigencies of his formal ideas demand. Shaftesbury also insisted that artistic genius does not imitate created nature: it imitates the creative genius of the universe itself. This is Shaftesbury's definition of the artist: 'Like that Sovereign Artist or universal Plastick Nature, he forms *a Whole*, coherent and proportion'd in itself, with due Subjection and Subordinacy of constituent Parts. He notes the Boundarys of the Passions, and knows their exact *Tones* and *Measures*; by which he justly represents them, marks *the Sublime* of Sentiments and Action, and distinguishes *the Beautiful* from *the Deform'd*, *the Amiable* from *the Odious*.'

This is not an attempt to force James into some invented tradition: rather I wish to suggest that in *The Sacred Fount*—and elsewhere—he was probing and exploring a profound aesthetic issue and that his notion of non-participatory speculation is related to the ancient and persistent idea of the artist as a man who creates forms which might be truer than the truth—the truth, that is, as apprehended by those immersed in the 'destructive element' seeking only to satisfy their 'provoked senses'. If his creations are lies, then they are lies not like truth, but better than the truth. The narrator of *The Sacred Fount* is at least eligible for Shaftesbury's definition of the artist as 'a second maker; a just Prometheus under Jove.' It is James's peculiarly modern insight—think of Mann's *Doctor Faustus*—to allow the suggestion that the activities of the artist might be allied to insanity. But then, who should have the last word on health in a disease-damaged world? Perhaps here we should recall the moving dying words of the artist Dencombe in *The Middle Years*: there can be little doubt that he speaks for James. 'We work in the dark—we do what we can—we give what we have. Our doubt is our passion and our passion is our task. The rest is the madness of art.'

E

V

The Voice of Scott Fitzgerald's Prose

ARTHUR MIZENER

I

SCOTT FITZGERALD's first book, *This Side of Paradise*, was published in 1920. It has considerable social and historical interest for, as Glenway Wescott put it, '*This Side of Paradise* haunted the decade [of the twenties] like a song, popular but perfect'. But except in this historical sense, it is not a good book; much of it was written and more of it conceived while Fitzgerald was an undergraduate. He revised it twice, at Officers' Training Camp at Fort Leavenworth in the fall of 1917 and in St. Paul in the summer of 1919, but much of this revision consisted of working into it stories he had written earlier. One reviewer, recognizing them, called the book 'the collected works of Mr. F. Scott Fitzgerald'.

Fitzgerald's adult work really begins, then, with the stories he wrote after the completion of *This Side of Paradise*. It has four fairly distinct periods. The first runs from 1920 to about 1928, when he wrote 'Outside the Cabinet-Maker's', the first story that clearly shows the characteristics of his later work. During this first period he lived with his winter dreams of success and happiness, though even then he was haunted by the döppelganger that appears in 'May Day' as Gordon Sterrett and keeps reappearing to the end of his career, when it is named Pat Hobby.

The second period of his work, which reached its climax with *Tender Is the Night* (1934), is a brilliant rendering of the almost sensual fatigue and grief of his gradual withdrawal from the world of these winter dreams, of the momentarily tender night that Charlie Wales and Dick Diver ('my comparatively good brother', Fitzgerald called him) live in before their final retreat to Prague or the lost towns of up-state New York, where they have to exist without either real or imaginary children.

In the two years between the publication of *Tender Is the Night* and 'The Crack-Up' (1936) Fitzgerald wrote little, and what he did write was not good. He was suffering a serious breakdown. The publication of the three beautifully written essays that begin with 'The Crack-Up' was the first sign—however much friends like Hemingway and Dos Passos disapproved of them—that the writer in Fitzgerald was coming to terms with his new situation, for, as he said in 'Pasting It Together', 'a man does not recover from such jolts—he becomes a different person and, eventually, the new person finds new things to care about'. It was this new person who began, with 'Afternoon of an Author' (1936), to write the quiet, intensely moving stories of the last period; and it was this person who was hard at work on *The Last Tycoon* (1941) when, on 21 December 1961, Scott Fitzgerald's heart literally cracked up.

In the stories he wrote after the completion of *This Side of Paradise* Fitzgerald began to discover and to express his deepest feelings, and in them we can hear for the first time what Lionel Trilling has called 'the voice of [his] prose', that subtle effect of precisely controlled syntax and rhythm, diction and overtone that can be heard when a good writer's prose exactly expresses the attitudes that constitute his permanent sense of life. Mr. Trilling describes the voice of Fitzgerald's prose as 'showing the tenderness towards human desire that modifies a true firmness of moral judgement'. He adds that this voice 'cannot properly be exemplified by quotation because it is continuous and cumulative', and that is of course true.

Nevertheless the voice of Fitzgerald's prose is the best measure we have of his sensibility at any given moment in his career, of the precise balance between his extraordinary gift for hope and his shrewd perception of actuality, between his admiration of grace and his rueful appreciation of the shoddiness of money-making, between his almost Renaissance love of fame and his awareness of the confused reality of success, between his understanding of love and his consciousness of the grubby actuality of mere sex, between his ecstatic delight in the fresh responsiveness of youth and his sharp sense of the fading of emotional energy with the passing of time. To listen to the gradual change in the tone of this voice, to see the paring away of borrowed, though often skilfully imitated tricks—for he was from the beginning an almost too skilful writer, a very quick student in the verbal tricks of his trade—is to get at the very heart of his work.

His sense of life was dominated by two complementary feelings. He was always aware of what Nick Carraway, speaking of Jay Gatsby ('my imaginary eldest brother', Fitzgerald called him), describes as 'the possibilities of life'. 'When I was a young man,' he once remarked, 'my own happiness . . . often approached such ecstasy that I could not share it even with the person dearest to me but had to walk it away in quiet streets and lanes with only fragments of it to distil into little lines in books.' Life without any belief in the possibility of such happiness was for him the life of the ash-grey men 'who move dimly and already crumbling through the powdery air' of that valley of ashes 'half-way between West Egg and New York' that is watched over by the huge billboard eyes of Doctor T. J. Eckleburg; when George Wilson kills Gatsby, Fitzgerald is careful to remind us that he is an inhabitant of this drab, colourless world—an 'ashen, fantastic figure'. But Nick Carraway is sure that the colour had already gone out of his life for Gatsby—that he had lost faith in Daisy, that his dream of a meaningful, happy life 'had broken up like glass against Tom's hard malice', and that 'he must have looked up at an unfamiliar sky through frightening leaves and shivered as he found what a grotesque thing a rose is and how raw the sunlight was upon the scarcely created grass'. Feeling this way, Gatsby chose to die. The dream, with the 'magical glory' it gives life, was that important to him.

But however much that 'magical glory' meant to Fitzgerald he was also always aware of how persistent and powerful the unmagical, habit forming routine of everyday life is. He saw that it begins by limiting the dream to its own meretricious materials and so making it an amusement-park paradise (he uses the image of an amusement park at the crisis of 'Absolution' [1924] as well as in The Great Gatsby). Moreover, ordinary life prevents the realization of even this dream, either as it did Gatsby's, or, more subtly, by exhausting the dreamer physically and emotionally, so that he loses his imaginative power to transform the world, as Dick Diver does.

For a man of Fitzgerald's temperament, this loss is a loss of the will to live; Fitzgerald's creative life from about 1935 was an effort to define an attitude towards living—or at least continuing to operate—after his will to live—or at least any of those romantic hopes that made him very much want to live—had been lost. Like the speaker in 'Afternoon of an Author', after 1935 he only very occasionally 'loved life terribly for a minute, not wanting to give it up at all', and he was speaking the simple truth when he wrote his daughter from Hollywood in 1938 that 'what I am doing here is the last tired effort of a man who once did something finer and better'; or, as he put it publicly in 'Handle with Care', 'I have now at last become a writer only. The man I had persistently tried to be became such a burden that I have "cut him loose"....'

But he could not sustain this attitude. Clearly as he saw the need for it, drained as he was physically and emotionally, well as he knew that the good life is always destroyed by the nature of things, the stupidity of the insensitive, or the dreamer's own tendency to slide from ecstasy into dissipation, he could never feel that living by the mean standards of ordinary life was endurable. Even in 'Handle with Care', he adds that 'just as the laughing stoicism which has enabled the American Negro to endure the intolerable conditions of his existence has cost him his sense of truth—so in my case there is a price to pay'. The price was not to like, or be liked by, anyone, 'so that life will never be very pleasant again, and the sign Cave Canem is hung permanently just above my door.' 'I will try,' he concludes, 'to be a correct animal though, and if you throw me a bone with enough meat on it I may even lick your hand.' Without 'romantic readiness' it was a dog's life.

II

The young Fitzgerald had experienced ecstatic happiness, but he had only a theoretical understanding that it depended on youthful freshness and would not last. Up to about 1930, the time of 'Babylon Revisited', what is fully realized in his stories is the glory of being in love with Judy Jones of 'Winter Dreams', or of living in the great, gay city he describes at the beginning of 'May Day' or in the joyous, innocent world of Mr. In and Mr. Out.

> Then they were in an elevator bound skyward.
> 'What floor, please?' said the elevator man.
> 'Any floor,' said Mr. In.
> 'Top floor,' said Mr. Out.
> 'This is the top floor,' said the elevator man.
> 'Have another floor put on,' said Mr. Out.
> 'Higher,' said Mr. In.
> 'Heaven,' said Mr. Out.

Inability to care about Judy Jones or to live in a city that 'had all the iridescence of the beginning of the world' or to ride towards heaven with Mr. In and Mr. Out was in this period merely an idea to him; he knew this idea was true, but it was something he could not yet feel.

The voice of his prose shows this quite clearly; it is wholly convincing when it is expressing Dexter Green's feelings about Judy, but it sounds forced when Dexter discovers, at the end of 'Winter Dreams', that he has lost his capacity to care. The best Fitzgerald can do with this feeling is to state it rhetorically—cover it with what he once ironically called 'blankets of excellent prose'; the rhetoric is skilful, but it is imitation and *appliqué*, not the genuine expression of a sentiment he has himself fully imagined.

> He wanted to care, and he could not care. For he had gone away and he could never go back any more. The gates were closed, the sun was gone down, and there was no beauty but the gray beauty of steel that withstands all time. Even the grief he could have borne was left behind in the country of illusion, of youth, of the richness of life, where his winter dreams had flourished.
> 'Long ago,' he said, 'long ago, there was something in me, but now that thing is gone, that thing is gone. I cannot cry. I cannot care. That thing will come back no more.'

The dividing line between the fully realized attitudes and the ones he could not find a wholly convincing voice for can be seen in the description of his not yet lost city in the first paragraph of 'May Day.' The romantic delight in the gaiety of New York in 1919 is clear and true, but the humdrum routine of ordinary life exists only as something scorned by romantic feeling, like the huddle of villagers behind the princely hero, a backdrop of the 'white-bunched faces' of 'merchants and clerks' whose daily life consists of some sort of inconceivable 'bickering and figuring'. The only 'merchants' Fitzgerald's early stories imagine sympathetically are wholly fantastic, like the one who, when asked by the heroine of 'Rags Martin-Jones and the Pr-nce of Wales' (1924) what he has for sale replies, 'Well, Mademoiselle, today we have some per-fectly be-oo-tiful love.'

By 1925 or 1926, the time of 'Absolution', The Great Gatsby, and The Rich Boy, the voice of Fitzgerald's prose has much greater range. It has often been said that the voice in Gatsby is persuasive because it belongs to a coherent character with a defined point of view, that we believe it because we believe in the character of Nick Carraway. But what makes us believe in Nick Carraway is the verisimilitude of his voice. The superiority of The Great Gatsby depends on a real extension of the range of Fitzgerald's voice, not just on a narrative device.

Despite the common sense, even the conventionality of Nick's attitude toward life, he is a sympathetic and sensitive man who 'reserve[s] all judgements,' knowing that 'reserving judgement is a matter of infinite hope'. However frequently we hear the note of ironic common sense ('Everybody I knew was in the bond busi-ness, so I supposed it could support one more single man') or even of flat conventionality ('I disapproved of [Gatsby] from be-ginning to end'), what we hear most clearly is the distinct, still slightly artificial resonance of his voice when he expresses his grief at Gatsby's defeat: 'It is what preyed on Gatsby, what foul dust floated in the wake of his dreams that temporarily closed out my interest in the abortive sorrows and short-winded elations of men.' The famous conclusion of Gatsby is similarly 'a little dramatic', as Mr. Trilling puts it, perhaps justly so. But the voice in *Gatsby* has very little of the merely mechanical resonance of the ending of 'Winter Dreams' ('that thing is gone, that thing is gone').

Much of the time, however, the book's images are still conventional. Like the grotesque rose and the raw sunlight on newly created grass of Gatsby's awakening from his dream, they are sophisticated versions of Fitzgerald's earlier images, such as the one in *This Side of Paradise* that describes Amory's mother as the product of 'a culture rich in all the arts and traditions, barren of all ideas, in the last of those days when the great gardener clipped the inferior roses to produce one perfect bud.'

But apart from the dramatic moments with their touches of rhetoric, the voice of *Gatsby* is quietly and reasonably moving. This is the voice we hear in the stories of this period, too. The voice of the opening paragraph of 'Absolution' (1924) is slightly raised by an irrelevant echo of the fairy story's voice: 'There was once a priest with cold, watery eyes, who, in the still of the night ...' but it is as a whole easy and natural. The passages of dialogue in which the moments of defeat are realized in both 'Absolution' and *The Rich Boy* are rhythmically controlled by feelings inherent in the stories as precisely as is the dialogue of the little poem about Mr. In and Mr. Out in *May Day*, although these are poems of deprivation and defeat, not of ecstatic joy. To compare the passage of dialogue in which Anson Hunter has to recognize Paula's happiness with the dialogue of Mr. In and Mr. Out is to see that Fitzgerald can now express disenchantment's vision as well as he can romantic illusion's.

III

By the end of the 1920's, when he was writing 'Outside the Cabinet-Maker's' (1928) and 'Babylon Revisited' (1931) Fitzgerald was living the disenchanted life a great deal more of the time. He was far from feeling yet that he had to cut his losses and bury his dead and come to terms with the colourless world of conventional feeling, but he felt much more vividly how formidable the Tom Buchanans were and how much weaker was the fairy's wing—

whose action is no stronger than a flower—on which the Gatsby world was built. His stories now depended much less on calculated rhetorical effects and their images were drawn directly from the events of the story, or at least fully earned.

Thus, when the father of 'Outside the Cabinet-Maker's' completes the fairy story that has absorbed his little girl completely, 'for a moment he closed his eyes and tried to see with her but he couldn't see—those ragged blinds were drawn against him forever'. The cadence of 'he . . . tried to see with her but he couldn't see' and the resonance of 'forever' are muted in this sentence, and the image of the blinds is taken from the story itself; these blinds hung at the windows of the apartment in which, in his fairy story, the Princess was held prisoner; they are magically transformed for his daughter, but they remain hopelessly ragged for him.

The ending of 'Babylon Revisited' is also concerned with a father's feelings about his daughter; it is even more beautifully restrained:

He would come back some day; they couldn't make him pay forever. But he wanted his child, and nothing was much good now, beside that fact. He wasn't young any more, with a lot of nice thoughts and dreams to have by himself. He was absolutely sure Helen wouldn't have wanted him to be so alone.

The 'forever' that is the nearly invariable signal of deep feeling in the stories of this period is now being thrown away; the rhythmical repetition that is so loud in 'Winter Dreams' has been subdued to the quiet, disguised paralleling of the first three balanced sentences; the forlorn 'so alone' is made nearly inaudible by the colloquial opening of the last sentence, which makes us hear Charlie Wales talking to himself rather than the author talking through him. Moreover, this thought really is Charlie Wales's; the night before he had dreamed that his dead wife had come to him and said 'that he was perfectly right about [their daughter] and that she wanted Honoria to be with him.'

A similar change has occurred in the normal narrative voice of Fitzgerald's stories of this period.

Charlie directed his taxi to the Avenue de l'Opēra, which was out of his way. But he wanted to see the blue hour spread over the magnificent façade, and imagine that the cab horns, playing endlessly the first few bars of *Le Plus que Lent*, were the trumpets of the Second Empire.

The cadences here are easy and natural, for all their intensity, and the images are earned, the creations of Fitzgerald's own feelings if not quite plausibly of Charlie Wales's—like the fine blending of the Opéra, Debussy, the taxi horns, and the Second Empire. (This passage was, incidentally, added to the story when Fitzgerald revised it for *Taps at Reville* in 1934.)

The voice of *Tender Is the Night* has the same ease and emotional power as the voice of these stories. Its opening paragraphs are representative. Their beautifully selected descriptive details create the appearance of the place and at the same time indicate the social values represented by that appearance—the way this nature has been methodized, by 'its English clientele' in the past, by the 'notable and fashionable people' of the present, and by the people of this story in between. The nearly indefinable impression that we are caught between the past and a future that has in historical fact already occurred is characteristic of the impressions that give these paragraphs their emotional force. Fitzgerald always responded strongly to what he calls, in 'Early Success', 'that all too short period . . . when the fulfilled future and the wistful past [are] mingled. . . .' The pattern of these impressions is delicate and complicated beyond description—the sensual pleasure of a place that promises a life of delight, a sense of pleasure becoming mere habit (after, as Dick Diver later says, the morale has cracked), the nostalgia for joy that one no longer feels but remembers vividly, and a great deal more. This quiet eloquence makes the one or two examples of Fitzgerald's older manner, with its extravagantly fanciful images ('deferential palms' cooling the hotel's 'flushed façade', and the 'bright tan prayer-rug of a beach'), seem almost crude. This voice is at its most brilliant in the account of the Diver's dinner party with its moment of ecstatic happiness as Dick Diver, an older Mr. Out, lifts the whole party 'a little towards the sky' by sharing with them his sense of the promises of life, and its moment of horrible everyday actuality when Violet McKiscoe, 'exud[ing] excitement . . . her mouth working a little' with her assurance of being on to a good thing, starts to report what she has come upon in the bathroom inside.

IV

The critical shift in the balance of Fitzgerald's feelings came in the middle thirties, when he surrendered his hopes that Zelda would get better, or that he could conquer the disorder of his own life or go on creating with any sense of glory. The voice of *Tender Is the Night* is dominated by despair at the everyday anarchy of Nicole's life with Tommy Barban and Dick's drifting across up-state New York, but this feeling is still balanced by at least a vivid recollection of the happiness of order and accomplishment. During the rest of Fitzgerald's career almost all one can hear in the voice of his prose is a wry acceptance of everyday actuality. The recollection of delight, of the pride of achievement, is there only as irony, as an implicit awareness of the loss this acceptance entails.

> I am very happy [says Forrest Janney, the drunken doctor of 'Family in the Wind' (1932)] or very miserable. I chuckle or weep alcoholically and, as I continue to slow up, life accommodatingly goes faster, so that the less there is of myself inside, the more diverting becomes the moving picture without. I have cut myself off from the respect of my fellow men, but I am aware of a compensatory cirrhosis of the emotions. And because my sensitivity, my pity, no longer has direction, but fixes itself on whatever is at hand, I have beome an exceptionally good fellow—much more so than when I was a good doctor.

This is the voice of a man who has measured the reality of his situation with complete objectivity and accepted it. Only the irony—'accommodatingly goes faster', cirrhosis of the emotions', 'an exceptionally good fellow'—shows that Dr. Janney, like the Fitzgerald of 'Handle with Care', remembers what he has lost.

This is the attitude that is expressed at the terrible moment when Mrs. King in 'The Long Way Out' (1937) comes down to the main hall of the hospital for the hundredth time 'in her powder-blue gown and her hat that looked like one minute after an April shower' to meet her husband, who has long since died. '"It's a beautiful day," said Mrs. King, "but of course even if it was raining it would be a beautiful day for me".' 'It's not a bad time,' as Dick Diver says quietly to Rosemary. 'It's not one of the worst times of the day.'

What makes this voice so moving is the suppressed impulse to believe again in achievement and happiness and the knowledge that to do so is to be as mad as Mrs. King is. As Fitzgerald says of Basil in 'Basil and Cleopatra' (1929), there was in him 'a persistence that was more than will, that was rather a necessity of pressing its own pattern on the world'. The old tension between accepted common sense and the dream that makes life significant and splendid is thus present in Fitzgerald's work to the end, giving his late work an undertone of grief that is all the more impressive because it never disturbs the quiet, reasonable surface of the voice with the slightest rhetorical tremor. This is the voice one hears in *The Last Tycoon*, for example when Cecilia, telling her story to the two men in the tuberculosis sanatorium. remembers how she felt about Stahr.

> Fresh as the morning, I went up to see him a week later. Or so I thought: when Wylie called for me, I had gotten into riding clothes to give the impression I'd been out in the dew since early morning.
> 'I'm going to throw myself under the wheels of Stahr's car, this morning,' I said.
> 'How about this car?' he suggested. 'It's one of the best cars Mort Fleischacker ever sold second-hand.'

—'Or so I thought.' Cecilia is going to throw herself under the wheels all right; she is really never given a choice. But they will not be the wheels of an adored hero's beautiful car but the wheels of Mort Fleischacker's best second-hand number, driven by the quite ordinarily sinister Wylie White.

This is the voice that tells us about the studio flood and the two refugees who found sanctuary along a scroll of curls on the bald forehead of the Goddess Siva; as they float down towards us and Robbie, the cutter, shouts: 'Put that head back! You think it's a souvenir?' Stahr sees 'smiling faintly at him from not four feet away ... the face of his dead wife, identical even to the expression'. It is the voice we hear when Prince Agge sees in the studio commissary the extra dressed as Abraham Lincoln.

This, then, he thought, was what they all meant to be.

Lincoln suddenly raised a triangle of pie and jammed it into his mouth, and, a little frightened, Prince Agge hurried to join Stahr.

This is the voice of Fitzgerald himself.

He went through the dining-room and turned into his study, struck blind for a moment with the glow of his two thousand books in the late sunshine. He was quite tired—he would lie down for ten minutes and then see if he could get started on an idea in the two hours before dinner.

He can still see the vision, even this late in the day, still be struck blind by the glow of life when the light for a moment falls right.

But he is quite tired, much too tired to try to live in the world of that vision. The only practical course is to save himself as much as possible and to work when he can. The voice is very quiet now, even casual—'Stick to your last, boy'—but, for all its quietness, deeply moving.

VI

Beasts and Politics in Elizabethan Literature

ANTHONY G. PETTI

MANY Elizabethan writers saw in the animal kingdom a valuable commentary on the nature and state of man. They had inherited from classical and medieval authors a vast menagerie of real and fictitious creatures, and often consumed their legacy with astounding prodigality. Sidney, in his *Apologie for Poetrie*, complained that 'in certaine printed discourses . . . all stories of Beasts, Foules, and Fishes, are rifled up, that they come in multitudes to waite upon any of our conceites; which certainly is as absurd a surfet to the eares, as is possible' (ed. Shuckburgh, 58). Among the biggest spendthrifts were John Lyly, who rarely could relate an incident without recourse to similes packed with creatures of various shapes and sizes; and Harvey, Greene and Nashe, who furthered their polemic battles by hurling a succession of bestial names at their opponents' heads. Spenser constructed elaborate beast allegories on the contemporary situation at court, and Shakespeare, whose plays contain over four thousand beast references, found animal imagery an effective method of character portrayal.

For the political and religious writers in particular, animals provided considerable advantages. The theorist could employ them to reinforce or exemplify his argument and to make his dissertation more palatable because of their intrinsic interest; and the satirist by means of beast fable or allegory was able not only to give his work a measure of artistic unity and objectivity, but also, in an age of severe press censorship, to conceal the forthrightness of his attack.

Apart from an obviously strong oral tradition, the numerous animal sources directly or indirectly employed for general analogy and allegorical framework included the Bible, the *Historia Animalium* ascribed to Aristotle, Pliny's *Naturalis Historia*, the works of Solinus and Aelian, the *Physiologi*, medieval bestiaries, and various physiognomical treatises from Aristotle to Giovanni Della Porta, incorporating an animal aspect of this pseudo-science. However, the most influential work was undoubtedly Aesop's Fables, which ran to many editions throughout Europe, at least sixteen of them being printed in England between 1484 and 1585. It was an extremely popular book for entertainment and educational purposes as Elyot testifies in *The Governour*. Sidney, despite his criticism of the abuse of beast stories, approved of the Aesopian method, whereby 'pretty Allegories, stealing under the formall tales of Beastes, make many, more beastly than Beastes, begin to heare the sound of vertue from these dumbe speakers' (*Apologie*, 20). Shakespeare used at least twelve of the Fables in his plays; and Nashe and Spenser were especially indebted to them.

Favourite sources for the orthodox political theorists were the medieval philosophical treatises dealing with the traditional ideas of cosmic order and degree, in which the animal world played a prominent part. These works were utilized in support of the monarchical form of government, to show that it was divinely approved. A typical example of this theory of degree is voiced by Sir John Fortescue (1396?–1476?):

> ... man is set over man, beast over beast, bird over bird, the fish over fish, on the earth, in the air, and in the sea; so that there is no worm that crawls upon the ground, no bird that flies on high, no fish that swims in the depths, which the chain of this order binds not in most harmonious concord ... nor from man down to the meanest worm is there any creature which is not in some respect superior to one creature, and inferior to another (*On the Law of Nature, Works*, ed. Clermont, I, 322).

More specifically, De Sebonde (d. 1432), in a passage of his *Theologia Naturalis* dealing with the hierarchy of angels, comments on the necessary existence of a leader in each order of creation:

. . . we see among the elements the fire the first in dignity; among the fishes the dolphin; among the birds the eagle; among the beasts the lion, and among men the emperor (Tillyard's translation, *Shakespeare's History Plays*, 16).

A hack writer for the Elizabethan government, Thomas Churchyard, summarizes this idea in a flattering tribute to the Queen entitled *Verses of Value* (1592):

> The Dolphin daunts each fish that swims in seas,
> The Lion fears the greatest beast that goes,
> The Bees in hive are glad theyr King to please;
> And to their Lord, each thing their duety knowes.

Opinion was sometimes divided over primacy in the natural world, the elephant being proposed as a rival candidate to the lion as sovereign of the beasts and the whale instead of the dolphin in the watery kingdom of fish, but the principle remained the same.

Because of the interrelation of the orders of creation, rebellion against the Lord's anointed was not only a heinous crime, but could also lead to serious disruption in the other orders of the universe. Shakespeare, who frequently gives utterance to the doctrine of cosmic order (*e.g. Troilus and Cressida*, I. iii 75 ff.), exemplifies the chaos in brute creation incident to usurpation and regicide in *Macbeth*, when, as a prelude to the murder of Duncan, the king's horses

> Turned wild in nature, broke their stalls, flung out,
> Contending 'gainst obedience, as they would
> Make war with mankind

and then fell to eating one another (II. iv. 16 ff.). The propagandist value of such a doctrine to the Elizabethan government was obviously very high. In the course of the reign it had to withstand two rebellions and one large-scale invasion (all abortive, it is true), and there was ever increasing religious and economic unrest. Plots against the Queen's life, both real and fabricated, were frequently revealed, while the question of her succession was always an aggravating problem. In addition, the democratic ideas of government which were gaining strength on the Continent began to have a firm influence on the Puritan party in England.

Among the important official publications to lean heavily on the doctrine were two constantly reprinted homilies entitled *An exhortation, concerning good order and obedience to Rulers and Maiestrates*, which originally appeared in the reign of Edward VI, and *An Homilie against Disobedience and Wylful Rebellion*, first published at the time of the Northern Rebellion of 1569. Both works draw on the animal world to demonstrate the necessity for order and obedience, and the second homily, which is an expansion of the first, opens with a description of the perfect accord which existed in the Garden of Eden, with all earthly creatures in their correct degree living happily under the dominion of man.

Churchyard, always ready to make capital out of political events or current governmental policy by exuding lengthy patriotic poems, was particularly fond of the theme of rebellion and its evils. In *A Rebuke to Rebellion*, composed in the year of the Armada, he delineates with copious imagery, in which the least reputable members of the animal world are liberally represented, the disruption and disease that the unnatural monster called insurrection brings to the normally healthy commonwealth:

> Rebellion is the Monster that I meane,
> A serpent vile that lives in stinking den;
> A griesly goast, a graceless spreet unclean,
> That lurketh close in shapes of vainest men.

By its machinations the lamb is matched with the wolf, the fox appointed guardian of the geese. The rebels are not hardworking bees but stinging wasps, 'scabbed sheep' among good ewes; they crow like bold cocks, but at the sound of a drum they hide like 'lyttle mytes, or maggots in a chees'.

An indication of the pictorial use of animal analogies of obedience and order in the body politic is provided by the lavish entertainment devised for the Duke of Anjou's arrival at Antwerp (1581–2). On a platform prepared for him in the market-place were represented, on the right, a lion holding a sword to signify the authority of the magistrate, and an eagle feeding her young

F

while turned towards the sun 'as taking hir force of the Prince';
and on the left, a yoked ox denoting obedience, and a hen guarding her chicks with a cock standing by, to represent 'watchful-
nesse, care, and defense of the superior' (J. Nichols, *Progresses of
Queen Elizabeth*, ii 379).

Because of the correspondence between the leaders in each
order of the cosmos, attributes of kingship were often described
by the characteristics of the animal rulers; for example, the
strength, courage and magnanimity of the lion, the nobility,
swiftness and clearsightedness of the eagle. Shakespeare's plays
provide ample illustrations of this usage. In *Richard II* the king is
likened to five other primates in the cosmos: the sun, fire, the
lion, the eagle, and the rose. When he sees Richard appear on the
walls of Flint Castle, Bolingbroke compares him to a 'blushing dis-
contented Sunne', to which York retorts, with a parallel simile:

> Yet looks he like a King: behold his Eye
> (As bright as is the Eagles) lightens forth
> Controlling Maiestie (III, iii).

The Queen, when she bids farewell to Richard before his dispatch
to Pomfret, tries to restore his courage by asking:

> . . . wilt thou, Pupill-like,
> Take thy Correction mildly, kisse the Rodde,
> And fawne on Rage with base Humilitie,
> Which art a Lyon, and a King of Beasts?

and receives the typically ironic reply:

> A King of Beasts indeed: if aught but Beasts,
> I had beene still a happy King of Men (V. i. 34–9).

The dolphin figures less prominently. In Shakespeare, the closest
it comes to kingly analogy is in Cleopatra's allusion to Antony's
'delights' as 'dolphin-like' (*Antony and Cleopatra*, V. ii, 108), and
in Talbot's pun on dauphin and dolphin (1 *Henry VI*, I. iv. 107).

The search for animal analogies to denote the special characteristics of successful rulers naturally moved much farther afield, and
drew in the qualities of various other creatures renowned for their
virtue, strength, wisdom or powers of survival. In chapter 18 of

Il Principe (1513), a highly influential, if misunderstood book in the Elizabethan period, Machiavelli, warning that a prince cannot rely entirely on being like a lion, adds as a requisite the special skill of the fox—hardly a noble beast, but one without equal for shrewdness:

> A prince must imitate the fox and the lion, for the lion cannot protect himself from traps, and the fox cannot protect himself from wolves (transl. Luigi Ricci).

A seeming parody occurs in Nashe's *Unfortunate Traveller* (1594), where the narrator, Jack Wilton, comments with mock seriousness that to be a successful politician and thus stand a chance of becoming a king, one must be like the wolf, drawing 'the breath from a man long before he bee seene': like a hare, sleeping with eyes open; and like an eagle, who, when flying, throws dust in the eyes of crows and other birds (*Works*, ed. McKerrow, rev. Wilson, ii 219).

During her reception at Norwich in 1578, Queen Elizabeth was given a 'monument', part of which, to signify two of her regal qualities, was engraved with the figures of a coiled serpent and a dove, and bore the inscription, taken from *Matthew*, X, 16: 'Wise as the serpent, and meeke as the dove' (Nichols, *o.c.*, ii, 154). The serpent was again used in one of an anonymous group of poems offered to the Queen as a New Year's gift in 1600, which, in attempting to show that in magnanimity, wisdom and beauty she surpassed all other princesses, paints her rather like an apocalyptic beast, with a lion's heart, a serpent's head and an angel's face (*o.c.*, iii, 471).

Beasts favoured to reinforce the picture of the Queen both as a second Virgin Mary and as a Christlike ruler of Church and State were the unicorn, symbolizing zealously guarded chastity, and the pelican, connoting self-sacrifice and devotion. Her attachment to the unicorn is exemplified by the fact that the horn of one, valued at about £10,000, formed part of the decor of her bedchamber at Windsor (Hentzner's *Journey into England*, ed. Walpole, 45). Among the literary sources is Matthew Roydon's elegy on the death of Philip Sidney, which alludes to the Queen as the 'maiden unicorne', in company with the 'burly Beare', representing Leicester, the lion, possibly Lord Burghley, and an unidentifiable elephant (*Phoenix Nest*, ed. Rollins, 9, 118). The legend of the pelican feeding its young with its own blood is adopted unblushingly by Lyly in *Euphues and his England* to demonstrate the Queen's spirit of devotion to the English nation (*Works*, ed. Bond, ii, 215); and the same sentiment is expressed in a verse epitaph which states that for the good of her people she 'Stickt not to spill, alas! her owne deare blood' (Nicholas, *Progresses of James I*, i, 11).

Easily the most frequently employed creature in this cult was the phoenix because of its sublime nobility and uniqueness, and because its self-immolation and resurrection paralleled Elizabeth's self-sacrifice and the perpetuation of her fame. Whenever the Queen's portrait was decorated with emblems, this bird was rarely absent. As instances can be mentioned a medallion, housed in the British Museum, bearing, on one side, the head of Elizabeth, and, on the obverse, a phoenix being consumed in flames; and a manuscript, preserved in the Bodleian Library, unctuously entitled *Hymne. A tres-haute tres puissante tres verteuse et tres-magnanime princesse, Elizabeth royne d'Angleterre* (1586), containing a full-length colour portrait surrounded by emblems, the top two of which depict the bird with a crown lightly perched on its head (E. C. Wilson, *England's Eliza*, frontispiece and opp. p. 244). The literary references are copious and extremely varied. They include George Peele's *Araygnement of Paris* (1584—'Live long the noble phoenix of our age'), George Whetstone's *English Myrror* (1586), and John Eliot's *Ortho-epia Gallica* (1593). The most lyrical utterance is probably Ludowick Lloyd's *A Dittie to the tune of Welshe Sydãnen* (1579), which contains the line, 'Sidanen is a Phenix fine'; and the most nonsensical, Thomas Churchyard's *Verses of Value* lamenting the flight of the royal phoenix from Hampton Court because of the plague (Nichols, *o.c.*, iii, 176 ff.). William Rankins, while satirizing English women in *The English Ape* (1588), tactfully excludes 'the Phoenix, endlesse in glory, and matchlesse in mortall maiesty'; the compiler of *The Phoenix Nest* wisely did not forget the compliment which the title of his miscellany implied to his sovereign lady and her court; and for Nicholas Breton, the defeat of the Armada provided an opportunity for an allegorical conceit 'Vpon an Eagle, and A Phoenix', in which the wondrous phoenix puts to flight the 'foule olde birde', Philip II of Spain.

The Spanish king was lucky to escape so lightly in Breton's poem, for there was a wide range of villainous and imbecilic creatures to draw on, far in excess of the virtuous ones. The Pope was normally a wolf usurping the role of shepherd, or the seven-headed beast of the Apocalypse, when he was not being termed the whore of Babylon; while Mary Queen of Scots, among many other things, was a venomous serpent. In addition to these, the most popular creatures to depict political enemies in invective or satire were the ape, the ass, the sheep, the fox, the caterpillar, the moth, the cormorant, and the buzzard—all noted for mental or moral shortcomings or for anti-social behaviour; though it should be noted that, since every animal, being created by God, had at least one positive quality, even some of these could be used occasionally to illustrate praiseworthy attributes—for instance the fox and the snake, as has already been indicated.

Englishmen involved in the dangerous game of satirizing their own government also called on the villainous beasts, but exercised a degree of caution according to their chances of being detected and punished. However, when it came to individualizing certain members of the Establishment, a special technique was normally employed in selecting the animals, based to some extent on the practice in medieval political literature, particularly the ballads and prophecies.

Of prime importance was the use of armorial bearings, in which the shield or badge, crest or supporters, normally included creatures of one kind or another. Perhaps the most famous example from the fifteenth century is the poet Collingbourne's use of the cognizances of Richard III and Lord Lovel in the lampoon:

> The Cat, the Rat, and Lovel or Dog,
> Doe rule all English, under the Hog.

Leading the field in the Elizabethan period is the white bear with the ragged staff, the Warwick badge derived from the Beauchamps, which was used by Robert Dudley, Earl of Leicester. Stone statues of white bears were proudly displayed in the gardens of the Earl's seat, Kenilworth Castle, and there are engraved representations of the animal in two of the works dedicated to him: Harvey's *Gratulationum Valdinensium* (1578), and Whitney's *Choice of Emblemes* (1586). Whenever the bear occurs as an obvious political reference, it is safe to assume that Leicester is intended.

Unfortunately, the same cannot always be said for the following heraldic representations of other dominant figures, for example: lions for the Cecils, the tiger for Francis Walsingham; the boar, the Earl of Oxford; the white horse, the Duke of Norfolk and the Earl of Arundel; and the dog or the hart for the Earls of Essex. Among the lesser personages may be mentioned the Earls of Westmorland and Northumberland, who were satirized according to their badges of the bull and the moon in W. Kirkham's *Ioyefull Newes for True Subiectes*, published in 1570, shortly after the defeat of their rebellion. The line of the nursery rhyme, *Hey, diddle, diddle* which runs 'the cow jumped over the moon' has been explained with much ingenuity but little evidence as meaning that Westmorland was able to escape while Northumberland was captured; or alternatively, it is suggested that the cow represents the Queen, since the dun cow was a heraldic bearing she inherited from the Earl of Richmond. (On the rare occasions that Elizabeth does appear heraldically or otherwise in a satire, it is usually as the lion, as, for example, in Spenser's *Mother Hubberds Tale*.) That readers of the satires actually attempted to identify personages by their coats of arms is borne out by Nashe's archly expressed complaint in *Lenten Stuffe* (1599):

> ... a number of Gods fooles ... haue fisht out such a deepe politique state meaning as if I had al the secrets of court or commonwealth at my fingers endes. Talke I of a beare, O, it is such a man that emblazons him in his armes ... (*Works*, iii, 213).

Puns also play their part in the beast disguise. In Collingbourne's couplet given above, they are made on the abbreviated forms of the names Catesby and Ratcliffe. At Elizabeth's court, a popular one was on Robin, a diminutive form of Robert, the christian name of two successive favourites of the Queen: Leicester and the young Earl of Essex, the latter actually using it in one of his despondent poems, where he speaks of the 'harmless robin' dwelling with the 'gentle thrush' (*Poems*, ed. Grosart, 95). The French envoy who wooed Elizabeth on Alençon's behalf was called by her 'the monkey', since he bore the name Simier (cf. Latin: 'simia'). Of the non-courtly puns should be mentioned Martin of the Marprelate controversy, the martin being a species of monkey; and of the non-beastly variety, Ralegh's christian name: Walter—water. Presumably the Bacons were obvious targets for this type of word play, but none seems to be recorded.

More fruitful even than armorial bearings for the political satirist were the nicknames bandied about the Court, most of them bestial. Just how well known these names were outside the Court is hard to tell, but there were probably degrees of obscurity. The Queen herself set the fashion. She seems to have been passionately concerned with surrounding herself with creatures of earth, air and sea. Her clothes were frequently richly embroidered with them, gowns, kirtles, stomachers and petticoats alike, a typical example being a kirtle described as 'aishe-colour cloth of golde, with workes of snailes, wormes, flies and spiders'. In the same list from which this is taken is itemized a set of 454 golden and pearl buttons shaped like tortoises (Nichols, *Progresses of Elizabeth*, iii, 501–12). Her jewellery, as exemplified by this inventory and by the catalogues of New Year's gifts dutifully presented to her reveal the same penchant. The phoenix, the pelican, and all the kingly beasts are represented in the jewels she received in 1574, together with the less significant parrot, falcon, salamander, hind, and mermaid. Leicester's present to her this year shows, as a symbol of his deep devotion, 'a lyon ramping with a white moseled beare at his foote' (*o.c.*, i, 380–1).

In giving beast nicknames to all her favourites, Elizabeth appears to have acted according to that strong mixture of sentimentality and cynicism in her personality which affected nearly all her love relationships as far as they can be ascertained. They are certainly strong marks of affection, but reduce their bearers considerably in stature, for they are of highly dependent, incapable, or uncomely creatures. Such is likely to be the case for a pre-eminently queenly sovereign with subjects for lovers, some of them easily young enough to be her children or grandchildren.

Her first 'sweet Robin' was also her lap-dog, rarely parted from her, as she once exclaimed to the French ambassador, De Foix (Strickland, *Life of Elizabeth*, 178). Her second was apparently a bumble-bee, who assumed the title in yet another despondent poem, *The Buzzeinge Bee's Complaynt*. Ralegh was a fish, and probably a goose as well, but most usually 'water'. His ascendency caused the jealous Lord Chancellor, Christopher Hatton, known as her sheep, mutton or bellwether (being the son of a sheep-reeve) to complain twice to Elizabeth in 1583 of the infiltration of a certain element into her affections. She assuaged him by replying that she would 'suffer no element so to abound as to breed confusion', that *pecora campi* would always be dear to her, and that she had always preferred flesh to fish (Strickland, *o.c.*, 339–41). Earlier, in a letter signed 'Your majesty's *sheep* and most bound vassal', the green-eyed Hatton had alluded to her affection for frogs, hinting at her suitor, the Duke of Alençon, termed 'the frog' by the Queen and the country at large, not only because he was a Frenchman, but also because he had the misfortune to resemble that creature. Elizabeth was so taken by the cognomen that she actually wore a jewel in the form of a frog with Alençon's face upon it, and caused frogs to be embroidered on her gloves (Strickland, 321; Nichols, ii, 248). Other known nicknames accorded by the Queen included sprite for Lord Burghley and crow for Lady Margaret Norris, one of her ladies-in-waiting (Nichols, iii, 75, 420).

In a court frequently torn by factions, the opposing parties, influenced by the Queen's usage, readily turned to beast nicknames as a weapon of ridicule and abuse. This was especially true of the last decade of the century when rivalries were at their height, the chief users being the followers of the Earl of Essex,

Leicester's successor as leading opponent of the Cecils—Lord Burghley, regarded by many as the real power behind the throne, and his younger son, Robert Cecil, who gradually assumed his father's mantle of authority. From Henry Howard's letters to Essex, it appears that Burghley was 'a toothles dog' or 'the old Leviathan' who with 'his cub' ought to be dragged from his 'den of mischevous Device' (B. M., Harl, 286, f. 268; Add. 4. 122, f. 78). However, his chief name, which, coming from his enemies, ranks almost as a compliment, was 'the old fox', as Essex himself called him. Burghley's unpopular, deformed son probably received more opprobrious names than any other Elizabethan or Jacobean courtier. The bestial variants ranged from James I's 'little beagle' to toad, the most usual being the ape, because of his lameness, meagre stature, humpback and practice of court flattery.

A less harmful creature, being generally sympathetic to the Essex party was Sir Thomas Egerton (later Baron Ellesmere), who figures as the dromedary in Howard's letters. There is, too, the spider, an unknown lady of the Court to whom Essex had a special aversion. As for the less polite names for the Queen, nothing is known for certain, but two suggested by seekers of political significance in nursery rhymes seem feasible: the cat and the cow.

Although there was usually a logical reason for associating individuals with specific animals—coats of arms, puns, vocation, physical or mental similarities—some beasts had to be chosen arbitrarily for reasons of greater security. This applied not only to printed works, but also to private letters, as when a cipher was required. An example is provided by the copy of an intercepted letter, now housed at Longleat in Wiltshire, seemingly written in the mid-1570's by a Catholic informer, who supplies a key to his animal cipher at the foot of the page. Despite the arbitrary selection of names, the title of fox for Burghley persists:

The names of our enemies.

The hare, the ladie Elizabeth that calleth herself queene; the foxe, Cicill; the slow-worme, Bacon; the newett, Knowles;

the spider, Sussex; the viper, Leicester; the snake, Essex; the lobster, Shrewsbury; the tode, Bedforde; the spiritt, Huntyngton; the mothe, Sadler; the penne, Mildmay; the otter, Clynton; the dogge, Williams, (Coventry Papers, lxxix, 84).

Of the English critics of the government, the Catholics could afford to be the most outspoken in print, for since their books were mainly published abroad, they were beyond the reach of retribution, yet could smuggle their works into England with reasonable facility. Though they were aware of and used the special conventions of animal substitution enumerated above, there was no need to conceal identities. As Richard Verstegan boasts in his *Declaration of the True Causes* (Antwerp, 1592), in which he ascribes England's troubles mainly to Nicholas Bacon and the Cecils, he had no need to copy '*Mother Hubberds* tale, of the false fox and his crooked cubbes' to attack the Lord Treasurer and his son, but could use 'plaine prose'. Thus, for Verstegan, as for other exiles, animal equivalents are for emphasis and embellishment rather than expediency. Whether it be the fox, or the serpent tempting Eve in the Garden of Eden (Eve being Elizabeth at the beginning of her reign) it is fully explicit that Burghley is intended; just as, in an earlier work on which the *Declaration* is partly based, John Leslie's *Treatise of Treasons* (Louvain, 1572), he is depicted, unperspicaciously, as a 'spitefull Pullet', a hen with a 'cakeling, ready and smoth tung', while his confederate, Nicholas Bacon, is the cock that 'trod' him.

In the famous Catholic onslaught against Leicester, *The copie o, a leter wryten by a master of arte of Cambridge* (1584), later reprinted under the title, *Leicestors common-wealth*, the writer (now thought to be Charles Arundel) uses general analogies such as the fox and the badger (pp. 18, 93) to describe the Earl, but also freely alludes to the bear cognizance to point and decorate his text. Early in the book (which is in dialogue form), the Gentleman comments:

You knowe the Beares loue ... which is al for his own paunche, and so this Bear-whelp, turneth al to his own commoditie, and for greediness thereof, wil ouerturne al yf he be not stopped or mouzeled in tyme (p. 13).

Farther on, in the discussion of the rebellion it was suspected Leicester would have raised had the Queen married Monsieur (formerly Alençon), the Scholar affirms his own loyalty by claiming he was resolved, by his lordship's leave, 'to folow Aristotle, who preferreth alway the Lyon before the Beare' (p. 210).

Among the extant attacks on members of the Establishment originating in the Court and circulating in manuscript, the most violent and explicit is *Letter of Estate*, considered to be the source from which *The copie of a leter* was derived, and perhaps instigated by Burghley. An especially interesting passage concerns the Earl of Arundel, then in prison for treason, and described as being in the bear's clutches. It relates that one day at table, Leicester fell to discussing crests, and in the course of the conversation,

> he, seming to be ignorante in that which hee knewe too well, like god Backus out of his cuppes of wine, demands what was the Earle of Arundel's creste, when presently one of his knaves makes answer, 'and it like your Lordship, the ramping horse'. 'Hang, hang', quoth hee, with an envius laughter, 'not much unlike, for as the horse that is wild and untamed will sofor no mann to mounte or tame hime, but kicke and flinge, sofering no man to come nighe him, but ready to lepp upp on every others backe, so the same horse beinge taken and tamed . . . becomes in short tyme so gentill . . . that any mane whosoever . . . sitt and ride him.' (P.R.O., Dom. Eliz., Add xxviii, no. 113, printed *Cath. Rec. Soc.*, xxi, 59 ff. See also *The copie*, 167).

Manuscript attacks which rely more closely on animal symbolism include two poems of the Essex party, written either by the Earl himself or one of his close supporters. In the first, the prosopo-poeic *Buzzeinge Bee's Complaynt*, said to have been composed about 1598 during his first discontentment and absence from Court (W. Devereux, *Lives of the Devereux*, ii, 194) Essex makes his complaint as a bee who, despite faithfully serving the King Bee (Queen Elizabeth) for 'ffiue years twice tould wth promases perfum'd', has received no favour but has been utterly rejected.

It was a time when sely bees coulde speake,
And in that time, I was a sely bee,
Who suckt on time, vntill my hart did breake,
Yet neuer found the time would fauoure me:
Of all the swarme I only could not thriue,
Yett brought I wax and honey to the hyue.

During his decline all other creatures prosper: 'Foule beasts' (the Cecil party) 'browse vpon the lyllys fayer'; all kinds of parasitic or destructive insects—the drone, the wasp, the gnat, the butterfly—succeed where he, for all his honest industry, fails; and even the 'fructlesse flye' finds a friend (stanzas 1-3). When he intercedes with the sovereign, he receives the laconic reply:

peace peevyshe Bee
Borne thou art to serue the time, the tyme not thee (3).
He has to feed on weeds when the moon is on the wane (the Queen withdraws her favour from him) while 'all the swarme in sunshine taste the rose' (enjoy the grace of the royal sovereign, the Tudor rose). Some animals pity him, some offer scorn, some merely muse, while others in envy, whisper to the king that he must be stilled and his sting removed (5, 6). Have bees suddenly become wasps? he asks; have bowls of honey become 'spiritts galle'? (spirit echoing the Queen's nickname for Burghley). Still he patiently awaits permission to suck a single flower (an office of state), yet upstart caterpillars are allowed to crop the plants that should by rights be his. Resigned to his fate, he utters a gnomic warning:

Moaths eate the cloth, cankers consume ye rose (10).

With a pun on the Devereux badge, the bee asserts that his heart, though sable remains a 'harte most true', but to no avail, for another enemy, tobacco (Sir Walter Ralegh) has stupefied his brain (12, 13).

A measure of the poem's popularity is indicated by the fact that it was set to music by John Dowland, though at a later date, when its topicality was dulled. It survives in several manuscripts, the text as commented on above being derived from a combination of the Tanner manuscript printed by Grosart in his edition of Essex's poems, and from a newly discovered source, the Melcome Regis Book in the Houghton Library, Harvard (f. 86) which contains some significant variants.

Immediately following this work in the Melcome Regis book (f. 87) is the second and politically more important poem, which has so far remained unidentified and unpublished. Like the first, it probably belongs to the early part of 1598, but might be later, if a possible reference to Burghley, who died in August 1598, in fact relates to someone else. With great bitterness it enumerates all the enemies of Essex, though not exclusively as beasts, relying principally on word play, clues to interpretation often being provided by strategically placed commas. The attack concentrates on Robert Cecil, who appears as the scheming Secretary (the office Essex had wanted so badly for one of his own followers), as a cub of the old fox with an apish will (the ape imitating his father's nature) and, in an atrocious pun, as Rob,art. Among the Earl's other pet aversions who figure are Henry Brooke, Lord Cobham, elsewhere termed 'the sycophant', and Charles Howard, Lord Admiral and Earl of Nottingham. A long-standing rival, at this time 'hande in hande' with Robert Cecil against the Earl, seems to be mentioned under his familiar cognomen, 'water', with a slighting allusion to his obscure origin. As in the first poem, Essex appears to be the speaker. A guide to the enemies he singles out is supplied to the right of the text, quoted here in full:

Admir, all weaknes wronge the right	*Lord Admiral*
honour in Generall, loseth light	*Generall : Francis*
Secret, are over their designes	*Vere ?*
thorowe whose dispite trewe honour pynes	*Secretary Cecil*
Awarde in worthe, wch is esteemd	
by vertues wrack must be redeemd	
Pryde, Spite and pollisie, taketh place	
In steed of Conscience Vallour and grace	
Noe Cob, am I that worketh ill	*Lord Cobham*
or frame my Tounge to envious will	*William Cecil ?*
Let noe man smyle at vertues fall	

Care we that list for I care not	*Sir George Carew*
by croked wayes trewe worthe to blott	
Nor will, I stand up, on the grounde	*Henry Neville?*
where such Impiety doth abounde	*John Stanhope?*
but basely Clothed all in Graye	*Lord Grey of*
vnto the Courte Ile take my waye	*Wilton*
where though I cann noe *Eagle* see	*The Queen*
A *Cub* is good enoughe for mee	*Robert Cecil*
whose mallice sorteinge to his mynde	
will frame his apishe will by kinde	
here may yo^w see walke hande in hande	
the Polliticons of this lande	
That Rob,art*es* glory wth a tounge	*Robert Cecil*
dipt in water from Limbo sprounge	*Walter Ralegh?*
These Buzardes mixt wth *Eagles* plumes	
to wronge true noblenes presumes	
Actions ffactions nowe we finde	
they that see not, are veary blinde.	

The poem probably contains a greater weight of significance than has been suggested above. If, for instance, 'Awarde in worthe' is a pun, it could relate to the fact that Essex had been Burghley's ward or to general injustices inflicted on wards by the fox as Master of the Court of Wards.

In this connection it should be noted that the Gray's Inn Revels of 1594, which often come as dangerously near to political satire as they do to obscenity, include a parody of the Court of Wards with quite a few references to foxes. These may not be as harmless as they appear, notably the allusion to black fox being a rich fur which can patch a lion's skin. The fox again features in the Revels in one of the 'neuter' apophthegms uttered by 'Paradox' which seems worth quoting because of the two examples already given in this article of the hare being equated with the sovereign: 'A hare is more subtill than a fox; for she maks more doubles than an old Reynarde' (Nichols, iii, 329, 340).

Turning to the political satires actually printed with licence in England, those of Spenser and Nashe, published in the 1590's, are outstanding for the degree to which certain members of the government, especially the Cecils, are individualized. Frequently forced to use the medium of beast fable and allegory, these writers sometimes had to disguise personalities to such a degree by an arbitrary selection of animals, that the point of the attack must have been lost on all but the highly initiated—the author's patron, an intimate circle of friends, and those with sufficient shrewdness to read accurately between the lines. Judging by the statements of Harvey and Nashe, the question of identification could cause almost as great a controversy as it does today (*Works of Gabriel Harvey*, ed. Grosart, ii, 54; *Works of Thomas Nashe*, iii, 213–14). For all their seeming obscurity, one wonders how such works ever passed the scrutiny of the licensers, unless myopia was induced by the bribery or influence of a powerful secret patron—in Spenser's case, probably Essex, the natural successor to his former great patron, Leicester, and in Nashe's, the Careys, especially Lord Hunsdon.

Nevertheless, the publication of the *Complaints* (1591), in which the bulk of Spenser's political beast satire resides, was short-lived, for it was quickly recalled, and with good reason. One of the poems in the collection, *Mother Hubberds Tale*, is an allegory, based on a popular fable, in which Reynold the Fox with his 'gossip', the ape, set out to better their lot. After various adventures, one necessitating the ape dressing up as an old soldier with the fox as his dog, they arrive at court and attempt to usurp the power of the sleeping lion who, awakened in time by a heavenly warning, reasserts his authority and punishes them. For its contemporary readers, the allegory, at least in the section on the court, was clearly an attack on Burghley and Robert Cecil under their familiar nicknames, and highlighted the way in which they attempted to rule the country, with the father encouraging his son to assume the outward authority while he retained the actual power. Because, as a blind to the topicality of the work, Spenser states in the dedicatory epistle that it was a product of his raw youth, some critics, thereby assuming it to date back to the beginning of the 1580's, have identified the ape as a composite Alençon-Simier figure; and the candidacy of Robert Cecil, comparatively recently proposed by Brice Harris (*H. L. Q.*, iv, 191–203), is still disputed. Other creatures in *Mother Hubberds*

Tale who may have political identity are the mule who gives advice on how to succeed at court; the sheep (Hatton?) to whom the fox had falsely promised friendship; and the tiger and the boar (Oxford?) who seek to destroy and devour the 'Camell' (perhaps the Earl of Arundel, since camel was another name for horse). The assembly of 'forreine beasts' are possibly the spies of the Cecils, and the griffins, minotaurs, crocodiles, dragons, beavers and centaurs can be taken to represent the various characteristics of their ignoble and unnatural adherents.

A more obscure beast allegory in the *Complaints* is *Muipotmos*, which tells the story of a handsome young butterfly for whom a cunning and malicious spider, acting like a 'wily Foxe', successfully prepares a trap. Of the multiple interpretations which have been suggested for this poem, that of Brice Harris (*J.E.G.P.*, xliii, 302–16) seems the most convincing, though the evidence he provides is by no means conclusive: it is an urgent warning to the young Earl of Essex to beware of the machinations of Burghley, who seeks his political destruction. Elsewhere in the *Complaints* one has not to look far to find other significant beast allusions. In the *Ruines of Time*, the first in the series, the poet, lamenting the death of his patron, refers yet again to Burghley, in this case as stepping into Leicester's shoes:

> He is gone, the whiles the Foxe is crept
> Into the hole, the which the Badger swept (216–17).

Later on, in the emblematic part of the poem he presents a badly needed vindication of Leicester's memory by a vision of two white bears, fairer than any other creature, lying asleep in a cave. They were not savage but gentle creatures, he claims, and had never craved for 'greedie spoyle' (561–74). By contrast, in *Virgils Gnat*, Spenser, speaking in the person of the insect, appears to rebuke the Earl (the shepherd) for casting him off, despite all the services he has performed for him.

Nashe is a little more cautious than Spenser in his use of beast allusion, for he either attacks dead politicans or carefully disguises the ones still living, and rarely allows his allegory to fit the contemporary situation in every detail. A typical example of his method is provided by *Pierce Penilesse his Suplication to the Divill* (1592), a pamphlet in the form of a long digressive letter to the devil in which many aspects of life in England are satirized. It was an extremely popular work, running to many editions, but damaged Nashe's career, for it alienated both of the major parties, not only satirizing the dead Earl of Leicester, but also frequently hitting at the Cecils—as in the isolated references to foxes ('*Raynold*, the Fox, may well beare vp his taile in the Lions denne, but when he comes abroad, hee is afraid of euery dogge that barkes'), and to the lions which they had obtained for their coat of arms.

The attack on Leicester takes the form of a fable, which has been skilfully interpreted by Donald McGinn (*P.M.L.A.,* lxi, 431–53). It concerns a bear (Leicester), 'chiefe Burgomaster of all the Beasts under the Lyon', who preys on all the other animals of the forest. After his attempt to overcome a 'fat Cammell' (Norfolk) has been repulsed, he enlists the services of an envious ape (unidentified), with whose aid he traps the animal and then devours it. Next, he poisons the deer (1st Earl of Essex), tears out the heart of the unicorn (Lady Lennox?) and causes general dissension among the lesser beasts. There is a second part to the fable, considered by McGinn to be a satire on the Puritans, in which the bear, yearning for honey, bribes the fox (Thomas Cartwright) to help him, who, in turn, seeks the collaboration of a versatile chameleon (John Penry) able to transform itself into an ape, a crocodile or a spaniel, according to necessity. While these two are scheming, the bear dies of vexation and grief over a hind that outruns him (the Queen, as McGinn suggests, or Leicester's wife, Lettice, formerly married to 'the deer', Walter Devereux). If, however, as seems remotely possible, the second part of the fable is entirely political, it can be interpreted as follows: Burghley (the fox) and either Walsingham or Robert Cecil (the chameleon) enter into an unholy alliance with Leicester for tricking the commonwealth (the husbandman) into destroying the nobility (the bees), so that they can appropriate the confiscated wealth and lands (the honey) and distribute the vacant titles among their own family, supporters and friends (the wasps). The plans of the conspirators are overheard by a spy (the fly) who reports what he has learnt to the Queen (Linceus) and they are thereby punished, as are the two animals in *Mother Hubberds Tale*, though in real life they escaped chastisement.

Nashe reaches much greater depths of obscurity in *Lenten Stuffe* (1599), in which there is a baffling beast allegory involving a falcon swallowed by a shark while attempting to catch a fish, a consequent declaration of war between the birds and the fish, and the election of the red herring as king. No satisfactory interpretation has yet been proposed for the fable, but to venture a wild guess, it possibly concerns the controversy over the succession to the English crown, with references to James VI and the Infanta Isabella of Spain.

The usage of beasts as exemplified by the poems of Essex and Spenser and the pamphlets of Thomas Nashe was so widespread that there appear to be instances even in the plays of Shakespeare, who rarely indulges in any type of political criticism. Whether he was responsible for them, however, or whether they were inserted by someone else, is difficult to say. In *Love's Labour's Lost*, an especially courtly play, there is a seemingly meaningless jingle concerning beasts in an interchange between Armado and Mothe (sometimes thought to be Ralegh and Nashe respectively):

Arm.   The fox, the ape, and the humble-bee,
          Were still at odds, being but three.
Moth.   Until the goose came out of door,
          And stayed the odds by adding four (III. i. 83 ff.).

In the light of identities already discussed, the riddle can be interpreted to mean that Burghley and Robert Cecil were at variance with Essex for political supremacy until Ralegh, who had been imprisoned in mid-1592 for seducing Elizabeth Throgmorton, was released (September 1592), and made up the fourth rival. If this interpretation is correct, the whole of the passage, if not the bulk of the play, can be dated 1592 or 1593.

The humble-bee and the goose reappear with apparently the same identities in the highly enigmatic play, *Troilus and Cressida*, in an epilogue perhaps added in September 1603, in which Pandarus, a Cobham-like figure, utters a little rhyme poignantly re-

lating to the Earl's loss of favour, the failure of his rebellion and
his consequent execution:

> Full merrily the humble-bee doth sing
> Till he hath lost his honey and his sting;
> And being once subdued in arméd tail,
> Sweet honey and sweet notes together fail.

Pandarus then laments his own downfall, resolves to make his will,
and, expresses the fear that a galléd goose of Winchester might
hiss—alluding not only to a particular type of venereal disease, but
also to the fact that Ralegh was to stand trial for his life at
Winchester, and might give evidence against him.

As this article has attempted to show, beast allusions can provide
a fine hunting ground for the literary historian, though a great
deal of circumspection has to be used. One must, for instance,
balance the exuberance of the enthusiast who sees a political
significance in every nursery rhyme ('A frog he would a-wooing
go': Alençon; 'I love little pussy': Elizabeth; Miss Muffet's
spider: John Knox) with the sobering remarks in the introduction
of the *Oxford Dictionary of Nursery Rhymes*. There is much game
to be captured, but the beasts are wily, suddenly slipping away to
leave the hunter to fall into his own trap.

BIBLIOGRAPHICAL NOTE

There is no comprehensive work on this subject, but the following,
which have been drawn on in this article, are among the useful subsidiary aids: W. M. Carroll, *Animal Conventions in English Renaissance Non-religious Prose*; E. G. Clark, *Elizabethan Fustian*; A. O.
Lovejoy, *The Great Chain of Being*; J. Nichols, *Progresses of Queen
Elizabeth*; A. Strickland, *Life of Queen Elizabeth* (a much maligned book
with some valuable sources); R. Taylor, *Political Prophecy in England*;
K. E. Thomas, *The Real Personages of Mother Goose* (almost entirely
lacking in evidence, but fun to read); E. M. Tillyard, *Shakespeare's
History Plays*; E. K. Wilson, *England's Eliza*; A. Yoder, *Animal
Analogy in Shakespeare's Character Portrayal*. The diverse interpreta-
tions of the animal allegories in Spenser are summarized in the

Variorum edition of the Minor Poems, volume 2. Some of my own interpretations concerning beasts in Spenser, Nashe and Shakespeare are contained in two articles in *Neophilologus*: 1960, 208 ff., and 1961, 140 ff., together with evidence on the identification of the bee and the goose.

VII

Two Clowns in a Comedy (to say nothing of the Dog): Speed, Launce (and Crab) in 'The Two Gentlemen of Verona'

HAROLD F. BROOKS

DESPITE warm appreciation of Launce as a comic character, it has often been denied that he and Speed have an organic part in the structure of *The Two Gentlemen of Verona*. According to Professor H. B. Charlton, for instance, 'Launce has no real right within the play except that gentlemen must have servants, and Elizabethan audiences must have clowns.'[1] This is to see the dramatic structure too exclusively in terms of plot.[2] There does appear to be only a single place where the behaviour of one of the clowns contributes to the progress of events; the critical moment when Julia, disguised as 'Sebastian', seeks service with her truant Proteus. Here, Proteus is influenced by Launce's recent misconduct: he is the readier to enlist the well-bred Sebastian because Launce has been missing for two days, and by the account he now gives of himself is proved too boorish to be entrusted with further missions to Silvia. Without question, dramatic unity is stronger when, as with Bottom or Dogberry, the clown impinges upon the romantic plot more obviously and decisively than this. There can be unity however, resulting from development of theme as well as from development of plot: when a play has a plot and themes, the *action* (which is what must have unity) may

---

[1] *Shakespearian Comedy*, 1938.

[2] I am confining 'plot' to the causal sequence; not extending it, with Una Ellis-Fermor in her fine chapter 'The Nature of Plot in Drama' (*Shakespeare the Dramatist*, 1961), to cover what she and Professor Wilson Knight call the 'spatial' pattern of a play.

be regarded as comprising the development of both.[1] Side by side with the causal sequence that carries forward his romantic plot, Shakespeare, in the parts he has given to Speed and Launce, is developing his play by means of comic parallels that illustrate and extend its themes. The parallels, as well as the causal sequence, are part of the organic structure.

They have not gone altogether unrecognized. '*Two Gentlemen* is . . . more integrated and patterned than has often been supposed,' writes Professor Danby in the *Critical Quarterly* (Winter, 1960); and although it is not his purpose to demonstrate the particular pattern I am concerned with, he remarks an item of it: 'Even Launce and his dog going through the pantomime of leave-taking translate the central seriousness into a comic mode.' The existence of the pattern, and half a dozen of its leading features, were emphasized by R. W. Bond in the old Arden edition (1906); he was the editor of Lyly, and familiar with the same technique in him. Had Bond's observation been fully accepted, and his fifteen lines on the subject been followed up, there might have been no occasion, by this time, to say more. But in the New Cambridge Shakespeare edition (1921) Quiller-Couch took no notice of them; and Professor T. W. Baldwin's reference, in *William Shakspere's Five-Act Structure* (1947), is sceptical, perhaps because he is thinking more in terms of characters than of themes: 'Bond, indeed, has suggested,' he writes, 'that each servant is a comic foil to and partial parody of his

---

[1] By 'action' I intend the total movement of the play, the enacted development of everything the play is vitally concerned with (story, situation, character, mood, theme, whatever that concern may comprehend), which conducts to the conclusion. So developed, and so concluded (even if sometimes the conclusion is deliberately inconclusive), these concerns, in good drama, are formed into an artistic whole, a whole greater than the unity of plot alone. The test of dramatic relevance is the contribution made to this larger whole, and the contribution may well be, not to the causal sequence, but to some other element in the developing pattern. 'Action' is perhaps the most variously used term in dramatic criticism. According to context, it can mean, for example: (1) 'business'; physical action as opposed to speech; (2) that part of the story which is enacted on the stage, in contrast with that part which is 'reported' or implied; (3) the events, especially the decisive events, of the drama, whether physical or mental, and whether occurring on stage or off; and perhaps (4) the designed sequence of those events, preferably, I think, called 'plot'.

master, but this appears true to me only in its most general sense.'

The themes in question are those of friendship and love, the first and second subjects of *Two Gentlemen*, which, as in *The Knight's Tale* and some of Shakespeare's own sonnets, are treated in relation to each other. The friendship is that which in Renaissance literature is constantly held up as an exemplar of noble life.[1] The love is courtly.[2] Julia, seeming at first full of 'daunger', soon reveals her 'pité',[3] and later sets out as Love's pilgrim. Valentine, like Troilus in Chaucer, begins as the Love-heretic, but quickly becomes the penitent votary. Proteus, from Love-idolator falls to Love-traitor, until reclaimed and redeemed from his treachery both to love and friendship by the sacrificial fidelity of his lover and the sacrificial magnanimity of his friend. Thurio is Love's Philistine, and the clowns, in this pattern, are Love's plebeians.

From Launce's first entry, each of his scenes refers, by burlesque parallels, to the themes of friendship on the one hand and of love on the other. Speed's scenes earlier, so far as I can see, do not depend on this particular sort of parallelism: Speed is not shown in burlesque roles as lover or friend, except momentarily, when he explains a piece of negligence, comparable to his love-lorn master's, by confessing he was in love with his bed. The scenes for the clowns are mostly built up from comic turns. Together, they play at cross-questions and crooked answers; Launce has his monologue of impersonations with the aid of comic 'props'; and Speed on his first appearance (I. i) has his mock-disputation (like Dromio of Syracuse) and his routine of witty begging (like Feste).[4] The episode, all the same, is not irrelevant clownage. It underlines at a single stroke both Proteus' friendship and his love: the friendship with Valentine has allowed

[1] Cp. J. W. Lever, *The Elizabethan Love Sonnet,* 1956, p. 164.

[2] Cp. M. C. Bradbrook, *Shakespeare and Elizabethan Poetry,* 1951.

[3] For 'daunger' and 'pité', see C. S. Lewis, *The Allegory of Love,* on the *Roman de la Rose.*

[4] Cp. L. Borinski, 'Shakespeare's Comic Prose,' *Shakespeare Survey* 8, 1955; and (on Launce and Will Kempe's slippers) J. Isaacs, 'Shakespeare as Man of the Theatre,' *Shakespeare Criticism 1919–35,* ed. Anne Bradby, 1936.

him to make Speed, his friend's man not his own, carry his love-letter to Julia. So, at the outset, a clown is linked with both themes. Speed reports Julia 'hard as steel'; thus preparing for the next scene of her metamorphosis to the compassionate lover. Proteus has exclaimed already:

Thou, Julia, thou hast metamorphis'd me;[1]

the motif is implied in his name, and belongs especially to him: yet Julia and Valentine are each to know metamorphoses, too. In the mock-disputation and its sequel here, this motif (as elsewhere in Shakespeare) is accompanied by imagery of human beings as animals. Speed (or alternatively Valentine) is a 'sheep', and he and Julia are 'muttons'. He is, moreover, a 'lost mutton', and in literal fact is in search of his master: he is in peril of failing to sail with him, a serious defection. The situation, then, and some of the backchat, are in keeping with a drama where defection, near-loss, and seeking are to be important: where Proteus' defection is almost to lose him his true self,[2] and cause him to be lost to Valentine and Julia; where Valentine is almost to lose Silvia, and the heroines must seek their lovers. Among the clown-scenes themselves, two others form a series with this one. Launce at his parting (II. iii) is likewise in danger of missing the ship, and is warned that he would thereby lose his master and his service. And his ultimate dismissal in favour of 'Sebastian' (IV. iv) echoes not only that warning, but Proteus' final comment on Speed here, that he is too unprepossessing a love-messenger and another must be found.

Some of these correspondences an audience will never be consciously aware of, though it will be affected by them. In the next clown-episode, in II. i, everyone sees the relation between Speed's humour and Valentine's high-flown romance. Speed comments directly on his master's love-melancholy. In taking over Valentine's former part as critic of love's absurdities, he helps to mark the metamorphosis:[3] the critic of Proteus' love has become vul-

---

[1] Quotations and references are from *William Shakespeare: The Complete Works,* ed. Peter Alexander, 1951.

[2] Well indicated by his sophistical argument to the contrary, II. vi. 19–22.

[3] 'And now you are metamorphis'd with a mistress' (II. i, 26).

nerable to similar criticism himself. The parallels are brought out
when Speed quotes him on Proteus and tells him he is blinder
now than Proteus was. As critics of love, Speed and Valentine
are not, of course, the same. With the eye of yet unconverted
scepticism, Valentine had seen its irrationality and its exactions;
with the plebeian eye, permanently limited though clear, Speed
sees its absence of practical common sense. In one respect, his
function is that of the Duck and the Goose in Chaucer's Council
of Birds, assembled on St. Valentine's Day. Love in the courtly
manner, partly because it is so stylized, is very liable, once we
entertain an inadequate, everyday view of it, to arouse mere
mockery and impatience. Aware of this, both Chaucer and
Shakespeare embody the dangerous attitude within the poem or
play itself, so as to control and place it; but they place it somewhat
differently. In Chaucer, the plebeian view, whatever sympathy
he may have with it outside the poem, is introduced chiefly to be
rejected. But when Speed protests that while his master may dine
on Silvia's favour, he himself needs meat, this is not 'a parfit
resoun of a goos': it commands sympathy within the ambit of
the play, and partial assent: it is one contribution to the complex dramatic image of courtly love that Shakespeare is building
up.

In contrast, there is the admired elegance of the device by
which Silvia confesses her love for Valentine. The dullness which
prevents his understanding it is a perfectly orthodox effect of
love-melancholy;[1] besides, as her true 'servant' he has too much
humility to be expecting any such confession. That so ultra-
courtly a gambit has to be explained to him by the uncourtly
Speed is humorous enough. And it is ironical that Speed should
do him this office of a good friend in his love, when his courtly
friend Proteus is soon to be his false rival. Diffidently blind here
in love, Valentine is to be too rashly and confidingly blind in
friendship. The theme of blindness and sight, especially love-
sight, is one of the most central in the play. It is because Proteus' fancy is bred only in his eyes, which until the dénouement see

[1] Cp., e.g., the Dreamer in Chaucer's *Boke of the Duchesse.*

no further than outward beauty, that he is altogether unstable.[1]
The truest praise of Silvia is that

> Love doth to her eyes repair
> To help him of his blindness.[2]

The theme continually recurs; and in the present scene the greater
part of Speed's cut-and-thrust with Valentine relates to it: 'Love is
blind,' 'if you love her you cannot see her,' and the rest, from
Valentine's question, on the marks of the lover, 'Are all these
things perceived in me?' to Speed's, on Silvia's 'invisible' stratagem, 'But did you perceive her earnest?'[3]

From Launce's entry, the relation between the clown episodes
and the leading themes, of love and friendship, becomes simpler to
describe; for it rests quite evidently throughout on the principle
of comic parallelism. One has of course to bear in mind that in
Elizabethan as in medieval work, burlesque need not mean be-
littlement of what is burlesqued.

The scene of Launce's parting (II. iii) is a counterpoise to the
high courtly parting of friends, with which Valentine and Proteus open the play. More directly, it is the humorous sequel to the
scene of pathos which it follows, the lovers' parting between
Proteus and Julia (II. ii). One phrase, on Launce's sister, 'as white
as a lily and as small as a wand,' is in the very idiom of love-
romance. Proteus has punned emotionally on the tide or season
of his departure, and Julia's 'tide of tears'; Launce puns out-
rageously on the tide and 'the tied,' namely Crab. At the end of
the lovers' scene, Julia, weeping, has made her escape in silence:
'Alas!' cries Proteus in his exit-line, 'this parting strikes poor
lovers dumb.' The clown enters in tears, but voluble, and in his
monologue re-enacts the weeping of all his kin. Crab's silence is
taken otherwise than Julia's; unaccompanied by tears, it is supposed to betoken hardness of heart, and gives his master great

---

[1] M. C. Bradbrook, op. cit.; and J. R. Brown, *Shakespeare and his Comedies*,
1957, q.v. for the whole topic of the lover's ability or failure to see beyond
appearance.
[2] Richmond Noble overlooks this (in *Shakespeare's Use of Song*) when he
finds the lyric comparatively lacking in dramatic relevance.
[3] See the passages in full: II. i, 29–71, 124–145.

offence. Attempting to identify the *dramatis personae* of the re-enactment with the 'props' available, Launce confuses himself completely, and in this self-confusion about identities the comic mode of his monologue chimes with what Professor Baldwin[1] has called the inward self-travesty of Proteus and the outward self-travesty of Julia, soon to be seen, and indeed with the whole theme of true identity and its recognition. The final claim Launce makes for his tears and sighs is likewise in tune with what is to happen. If he did miss the tide, he declares, they would float him and waft him to overtake Proteus. To overtake Proteus is just what Julia's love-sorrow, of which they are the comic counter-parts, will shortly impel her to do.

The reunion of Launce and Speed in Milan (II. v) immediately succeeds that of the friends, their masters; and their dialogue comments on the love-theme. It is certain, Launce tells his com-rade, that it will be a match between Proteus and Julia. Proteus has just left the stage soliloquizing on his change of allegiance, and is about to return resolving to court Silvia as though Julia were dead. Yet in the end, Launce will prove right after all. Again, he furnishes a comic reminder of the discretion proper in com-municating love-secrets even to the bosom-friend. His display of caution ('Thou shalt never get such a secret from me but by parable') contrasts with Valentine's indiscreet disclosure to Proteus of the plans for his elopement, a disclosure made in the previous scene (II. iv). In the next (II. vi) Proteus determines on betraying his friend's confidence to the Duke. His entry alone, meditating this treachery, is set against the amicable exit of Speed and Launce, going off 'in Christian charity' to drink together.

The episode of Launce and his letter (which ends III. i) affords even more striking parallels with both the love and friendship themes. It evokes comparison with the two romantic letter-scenes earlier (I. ii, II. i): Julia receiving Proteus' love-letter, and Silvia giving Valentine the love-letter she has made him write on her behalf. In burlesque contrast with Julia's emotion and Silvia's graceful device, Launce's letter is a step towards a bargain in the

[1] Op. cit.

marriage-market. It is a report from a go-between on the merits and demerits of his intended; and on the strength of it he makes up his mind to have her, because though toothless she is well-off. This love-transaction, which is not pursued in the courtly way, by courtship of the lady, and which is clinched by mercenary considerations, clean against the canon of true love, casts a light on the next scene (III. ii) and its sequel (IV. ii). Here, by the courtliest kind of courtship—a serenade—but no less against the canon of true love, the assault upon Silvia's loyalty to Valentine is planned on behalf of the foolish Thurio, whom her father prefers for his wealth, and is used by the faithless Proteus as cover for his own pursuit of her. Beside the moral deformity of Proteus' conduct in love, the comic deformity of Launce's is as nothing.

When the letter-episode begins, we have just seen Valentine banished, in consequence of having enlisted Proteus' counsel about the elopement. Launce soliloquizes on Proteus' knavery, and his own secrecy: 'I love . . . but what woman I will not tell myself'—burlesquing at once the code and Valentine's breach of it. Then, like Valentine, he enlists a confidant; and like Proteus, betrays his friend. He cajoles Speed into helping him read the letter, and rejoices that Speed will earn a beating by it. Though the roles are switched (since the confidant, not the confider, is betrayed), the parallel is clear.

Launce's last monologue, just before his dismissal by Proteus and from the play (IV. iv), is of course his tale of Crab's crimes at court, with his own quixotic devotion and fidelity to the ungrateful, ill-conditioned cur. It comes almost straight after Proteus' nocturnal courtship of Silvia, in triple treachery to Julia, Valentine, and Thurio; and between the arrival of Julia in her devotion and fidelity, only to witness this treachery of his (IV. ii), and her taking service with him (in IV. iv), ungrateful and ill-conducted as she has found him. 'When a man's servant shall play the cur'—so Launce starts his complaint of Crab, and so Proteus might complain of Launce himself, 'who still . . . turns [him] to shame.' But we have heard this word 'servant' repeated in the sense of 'courtly lover': what when a lady's 'servant' shall play the cur?

Yet Julia does not refuse the quixotic task of bearing Proteus' love-plea to her unwilling rival.[1]

I am hinting a comparison of Proteus with Crab; and I do not think it extravagant, provided one is not too serious about it, to see reflected in Crab, comically and a little pathetically, the transgressor in Proteus. The want of sensibility to old ties and to his friend Launce's feelings which Crab is alleged to show at parting from home, is ominous as a parallel to Proteus' parting from Julia and impending reunion with Valentine. As a present for Silvia, Crab resembles the love that Proteus proffers her. He is a sorry changeling for the true love gift Proteus meant to bestow. He is unfit for Silvia (persecuting her with most objectionable attentions!), and offensive where true courtliness should rule. Like Proteus, he gets his friend into trouble. And as Crab is only saved by Launce's quixotic, self-sacrificial affection, so Proteus is only saved by the extremes to which Valentine is ready to carry his friendship and Julia her love. From them Proteus learns his lesson. As in *Love's Labour's Lost*, an opening debate in which love and education were pitted against each other has led into a drama of education in and through love. The theme of education is touched occasionally in the earlier clown-scenes (Speed has been corrected for inordinate love—of his bed), but it appears more plainly when Launce reproaches Crab: 'did I not bid thee still mark me, and do as I do?' Crab cannot learn; but Proteus learns the value of constancy from the example and reproaches of Julia, Valentine, and Silvia.[2] Whether Crab says ay or no, and whatever the antics of Proteus the trangressor,[3] it is a match between the regenerate Proteus and his Julia. Yet with all this, Crab is the clown's dog, not a symbol or a piece of allegory: I mean simply to suggest that the impression the dog makes on an audience has this various aptness to the main action and its themes.

[1] Though it must be admitted that, unlike Viola, she doesn't propose to put her heart into it.

[2] Cp. Harold Jenkins, 'Shakespeare's *Twelfth Night*', *The Rice Institute Pamphlet*, xlv. 4, Jan. 1959.

[3] 'If he say ay, it will; if he say no, it will; if he shake his tail and say nothing, it will.' (II. v, 31).

The structural use of parallels between main and subsidiary actions, in conjunction with plot or otherwise, is not infrequent in our drama. In subsequent plays of Shakespeare's there are many examples. Hal's interview with his father is rehearsed beforehand in Eastcheap, and Malvolio, no less than Orsino and Olivia, cherishes an illusory ideal of love. The underplot of *The Changeling* owes its relevance to the same technique. But while Bond was right to discern it in *Two Gentlemen*, he was in error when he traced it solely to Lyly. It was not initiated, as he seems to have thought, by *Endimion*: it unites the comic and serious actions in the *Secunda Pastorum*, (*c.* mid-fifteenth century) and in *Fulgens and Lucres* (*c.* 1500). It is not confined to plays 'in two tones'; the most famous instance of all is the double plot of *King Lear*. It is something to look for before assessing a dramatist's construction. Congreve's intrigue-plots are not among the finest features of his art, but he is a master of construction in parallel, witness the successive quarrel-scenes in the second Acts of *Love for Love* and *The Way of the World*; and the fourth Act of the latter, made up of contrasted wooings. In Shaw's *Major Barbara*, the organic contribution of the first episode is better appreciated when we recognize the parallelism of theme: the play is about different kinds of power, and the opening shows the sort of power Lady Britomart wields in her household. Similarly, to look at the use of parallels in *The Two Gentlemen of Verona* alters our estimate of its construction.

VIII

Of the Right Use of Riches

KEITH W. SALTER

I cannot call riches better than the baggage of virtue. The Roman word is better, *impedimenta*. For, as the baggage is to an army, so is riches to virtue. It cannot be spared nor left behind, but it hindereth the march; yea and the care of it sometimes loseth or disturbeth the victory. Of great riches there is no real use, except it be in the distribution; the rest is but conceit. So saith Solomon: *Where much is, there are many to consume it; and what hath the owner but the sight of it with his eyes?* The personal fruition in any man cannot reach to feel great riches: there is a custody of them or a dole and donative of them or a fame of them but no solid use to the owners.

Francis Bacon in writing these words was giving expression to one of the great commonplaces of moral teaching, but there is no need to be apologetic for re-introducing this commonplace in our present situation; indeed, in the modern world there is a powerful and dangerously tacit assumption that the acquisition of money, as of leisure, is so self-evidently desirable that it need not really be discussed, still less questioned, at all. There is surely a need for an examination of these assumptions as well as of the explicit declarations of our political leaders today. In the last general election in this country, spokesmen of all parties in their various promises and offers all seemed to assume that an increase in what is called the standard of living is what everyone wants and is what will, of necessity, conduce to our happiness. There is very little public discussion today of what may be called the quality of our living or of the conditions which really concern the precise nature of our happiness. What, for instance, are we to say is the modern word for Bacon's 'virtue'? How are we to frame in terms proper to the life of the truly human individual the relevant answer to the invitation to rejoice in the prospect of doubling the standard of living in the next twenty-five years? What indeed *are* the standards of living in terms of a truly civilized way of life? The life which is to be lived in the individual and in his relationship with other individuals or else nowhere—which is revealed, as D. H. Lawrence has said, in 'sensitive life rather than in inventions'.

There are two powerful words which are relevant to these questions—'justice' and 'naturalness'. The notions expressed by these words have long been the targets for, but resist, precise definition. We can read in Aquinas that justice is 'the perpetual and constant will to render to each one his right' (*Summa* 2. 2. 66. 1), but for an answer to what this may mean in terms of specific human situations we will be well advised to turn to literature, although the difficulties of an intellectual formulation remain unsurmounted. King Lear, when for the first time in his life he is brought up against actual material deprivation, is appalled by his own ignorance of conditions which he ought as a responsible ruler to have known:

> O! I have ta'en
> Too little care of this. Take physic, Pomp;
> Expose thyself to feel what wretches feel,
> That thou mayst shake the superflux to them
> And show the Heavens more just.

These words can bear a more than personal weight; they support a truth which goes beyond the response by a single character to a hitherto unrealized experience, and Shakespeare takes care to repeat this crucial idea when Gloucester, physically blinded but morally awakened, echoes Lear's cry:

> Let the superfluous and lust-dieted man,
> That slaves your ordinance, that will not see
> Because he does not feel, feel your power quickly;
> So distribution should undo excess
> And each man have enough.

Both these passages sustain Bacon's doctrine that the right use of wealth must lie in its fair distribution. Lear's words go further:

that it is man who must act as an agent of Heaven's justice in ordering this right distribution. The words 'shake the superflux to them' carry in them a feeling of the ripe fruits of the earth to be harvested from the orchard trees which are the endowment of Nature, to be shared by all. The doctrine implied here is the very antithesis of what the economists and philosophers of a later period and of our time call *laissez-faire*. It is, rather, an expression of the traditional doctrine of stewardship that the fruits of the earth are in our trust, not our possession, and that the distribution of wealth is or should be a moral concern: it is we who must show the Heavens more just, not leave things to the natural play of economic forces, as the modern phrase has it, or to a Providence which will act directly without human agency.

But how are we to agree on what is enough for each man so that Heaven shall be shown to be just? What is it to render to each one his right? The Marxist has, presumably, no difficulty in answering this question theoretically, but the problem of defining what are indeed human needs goes beyond the satisfaction of material necessities and their fair distribution, fundamental though these problems are. Can we withhold assent from Lear's protest against the rationality of Regan when she questions the need for the old King to be attended by even five and twenty men?

> O! reason not the need; our basest beggars
> Are in the poorest thing superfluous:
> Allow not Nature more than Nature needs,
> Man's life is cheap as beast's. Thou art a lady;
> If only to go warm were gorgeous,
> Why, Nature needs not what thou gorgeous wear'st,
> Which scarcely keeps thee warm.

I take this passage to have as one of its complex meanings the sense that man's true needs are other than the satisfaction of animal requirements; he is even prepared to forgo a degree of physical comfort if his further demands are satisfied, that the satisfaction of nature's needs are not enough. We seek, that is, a standard of human naturalness which refers to needs other than those which we have in common with other animals. There is a truth in

Chesterton's remark that if you give me the luxuries of life I will dispense with the necessities. On the other hand an excessive pursuit of luxury which blinds a man to his natural being, to his physical limitations, can itself bring him to a less than humanly natural level, may indeed become profoundly destructive.

Medieval Christian doctrine, inheriting and incorporating an earlier wisdom, saw money as good not in itself but as enabling a man to be properly himself, to live up to his specifically human stature. What this standard of human nature was, depended and depends on assumptions which must ultimately be called religious, that is, on the beliefs in which you put your trust and which make life worth living for you. Ben Jonson for instance is drawing upon a classical tradition of the natural mean in the passage I quote next; but what he writes is put, as it were, as an article of faith. It embodies a tough popular wisdom of the kind that anyone who has participated in the daily risks of total war will recognize as authentic, and which our present situation needs as an instrument of practical politics. It involves the necessity of recognizing and facing the presence of death and the inevitability of change, of daily change. This recognition is a crucial step in arriving at a working definition of human naturalness, a definition which we must make if an answer to the question 'what is enough?' is to be offered at all.

> who can endure to see
> The fury of men's gullets, and their groins?
> What fires, what cooks, what kitchen might be spared?
> What stews, ponds, parks, coops, games, magazines,
> What velvets, tissues, scarfs, embroideries,
> And laces they might lack? They covet things
> Superfluous still; when it were much more honour
> They could want necessary: what need hath nature
> Of silver dishes or gold chamber-pots?
> Of perfumed napkins, or a numerous family
> To see her eat? poor and wise, she requires
> Meat only; hunger is not ambitious:
> Say, that you were the emperor of pleasures,
> The great dictator of fashions, for all Europe,

And had the pomp of all the courts, and kingdoms,
Laid forth unto the show, to make yourself
Gazed and admired at; You must go to bed
And take your natural rest; then all this vanisheth,
Your bravery was but shewn; 'twas not possest:
While it did boast itself, it was then perishing.
                              The Staple of News III. ii.

The paradox that we cannot avoid here is that whereas these
superfluities are strictly unnecessary for our natural rest or relief
it is also a part of human nature to desire them. An implication
that can be drawn from this passage is that we can legitimately
enjoy these indulgences provided that we do not regard them as
indispensable, that we are not committed to them ('we must stand
aside', says D. H. Lawrence). It is however a common experience
that luxuries very soon come to be regarded as necessities. We
need therefore a reminder that we own nothing in perpetuity,
indeed that we have no absolute possessions at all: we need, that
is, an image of stewardship, just as we need an image of death, for
the construction of our standard of human naturalness. The
possession of riches involves responsibilities which cannot be
measured in monetary terms. This traditional wisdom was
slowly disappearing from literary expression in the course of the
seventeenth century in England, but Pope in a passage written
some hundred years after Ben Jonson's death shows his possession
of it firmly and positively. He is considering Timon's cold pomp
and the barren, self-regarding splendour to which riches, without
the human standard we are seeking to define, will make us victims:

But hark! The chiming clocks to dinner call;
A hundred footsteps scrape the marble hall:
The rich buffet well colour'd serpents grace,
And gaping Tritons spew to wash your face.
Is this a dinner, this a genial room?
No, 'tis a temple, and a hecatomb.
A solemn sacrifice perform'd in state,
You drink by measure, and to minutes eat.
So quick retires each flying course, you'd swear
Sancho's dread doctor and his wand were there.

Between each act the trembling salvers sing,
From soup to sweet-wine, and God bless the King.
In plenty starving, tantaliz'd in state,
And complaisantly help'd to all I hate,
Treated, caress'd, and tir'd, I take my leave,
Sick of his civil pride from morn to eve;
I curse such lavish cost, and little skill,
And swear no day was ever past so ill.

Yet hence the poor are cloth'd, the hungry fed;
Health to himself, and to his infants bread
The labourer bears: what his hard heart denies
His charitable vanity supplies.

Another age shall see the golden ear
Imbrown the slope, and nod on the parterre,
Deep harvests bury all his pride has plann'd
And laughing Ceres re-assume the land. . . .

Epistles to Several Persons, IV.

Consider how Pope communicates his judgements here: 'Treated, caress'd . . .' We treat a child, we caress a lap dog. We resent the implication that because Timon is rich he can therefore treat us as less than adult or as items for his own amusement or display. The whole passage implies that the humanity, which Timon lacks here, lies in an awareness of and respect for human beings as other and separate persons. We must not use our fellow beings as extensions of our own selfhood or as private possessions to be made the objects of arrangement or disposal.

It is with a sense of relief, of a justice achieved, that we read the last four lines. The rightful owner will take over, will redeem this elaborate and costly waste:

Deep Harvests bury all his pride has plann'd
And laughing Ceres re-assume the land . . .

But the rightful owner is not the human figure; it is the goddess, a positive, affirmative power which we can reverence and with whom we should work in delight and service. The word which we must now add to our store is 'humility'. It is easy to write or speak the word; but what *is* humility in terms of the activities of the economist, the financier, the engineer or the politician?

It may be useful here to reflect on what was happening between the time when Shakespeare and Jonson were writing and Pope's day. Lear and Gloucester both say that they must feel what other people feel; in particular, what the poor feel. The 'lust-dieted and superfluous man' will not see because he does not feel. Lear exclaims that Edgar in the extreme of poverty represents a reality; 'thou art the thing itself': and seeks to identify himself with this reality, and begins tearing off his clothes. We see here perhaps a dramatic presentation of an area of human experience which in traditional religious terms is called 'holy poverty'. Of all the notions I am hinting at it is perhaps the most removed from present western society. Let us consider though, for a moment, one of the changes in attitudes towards poverty in the seventeenth century. During this period the word 'poverty' tends to become almost exclusively an economic term; a term, too, which implies disgrace. The poverty of Chaucer's parson was no disgrace, and deprivation and nakedness in Lear are the conditions of a truer insight. My next quotation is from a play which appeared in 1707. The tone is admittedly bantering and ironic but the dialogue is handling, I would claim, social assumptions that were powerful. The two speakers, Archer and Aimwell—the play is Farquhar's *Beaux Stratagem*—are saying that nowadays it is a crime to be without money: 'There is no scandal like rags. . . . Men must not be poor: idleness is the root of all evil; the world's wide enough, let 'em bustle. Fortune has taken the weak under her protection, but men of sense are left to their industry.' I suggest that the memory of the older doctrine that the love of money is the root of all evil was not yet too faint for the joke not to be disturbing. Let Fortune look after the weak, the man of sense will take his opportunities when and where he can: Heaven will reward industry and unaided effort. The poor will have only themselves to blame; they must take their chance. Lear's cry is only faintly audible now. Where is the justice now that men must administer to show that Heaven is indeed just? The change in attitude towards the poor is relevant to our topic because it reveals a weakening in the concepts of a just distribution. To quote briefly from a sermon of Latimer will illustrate the older doctrine: 'The poor man hath title to the rich man's goods: so that the rich man ought to let the poor man have part of his riches to help and comfort him withal.' These are also Lear's words. The poor must not be despised; indeed a kind of reverence is owing to them. Christ was poor and outcast.

At the end of the seventeenth century we find that religious opinion perhaps more so than popular opinion was putting less emphasis on the obligation of charity than upon the duty of work. The Puritans are made fun of in Restoration drama but a Puritan doctrine would seem to have won; the doctrine that practical success is at once the sign and the reward of ethical superiority. If you believe this, you will not pity the poor or, if you do, it will be with a kind of contempt: 'Let 'em bustle', they are idle fellows. If we look again at Farquhar's *Beaux Stratagem* we find a sneer at the traditional care for the poor which Lady Bountiful exercises. The sneer comes from the sophisticated city Lady who is her daughter, Mrs. Sullen. An old countrywoman seeking help for her husband, who is ill, mistakes Mrs. Sullen for her mother.

> *Woman:* I come, an't please your ladyship—you're my Lady Bountiful, an't ye?
>
> *Mrs. Sullen:* Well, good woman, go on.
>
> *Woman:* I have come seventeen long mile to have a cure for my husband's sore leg.
>
> *Mrs. Sullen:* Your husband! What, woman, cure your husband!
>
> *Woman:* Ay, poor man, for his sore leg won't let him stir from home.
>
> *Mrs. Sullen:* There, I confess, you have given me a reason. Well good woman, I'll tell you what you must do. You must lay your husband's leg upon a table, and with a chopping-knife you must lay it open as broad as you can, then you must take out the bone, and beat the flesh soundly with a rolling pin, then take salt, pepper, cloves, mace, and ginger, some sweet herbs, and season it very well. Then roll it up like brawn, and put it into the oven for two hours.
>
> *Woman:* Heavens reward your ladyship!
>
> *The Beaux Stratagem*, IV. i.

Fortunately the real Lady Bountiful arrives in time. Admittedly Mrs. Sullen is preoccupied with her own misfortunes; she is married to a drunken boor of a squire; but I do not think we would find in Elizabethan drama a joke which involved the idea of the responsibilities of the rich towards the weak.

How can this be related to our attempt to suggest what makes for human naturalness? Perhaps two points emerge; first that we should seek to understand anew what is meant by Puritanism and the Puritan's attitude to money and to scrutinize what we find in order to see its relation with the older tradition of our civilization or what remains of it. (This would involve us, for example, in a re-reading of Dickens's *Hard Times* from a viewpoint not entirely that which Dr. Leavis takes.) Second: we must feel with Dr. Johnson the vanity of human wishes and share the compassion he conveys for those to whom his phrase 'the insufficiency of human enjoyments' is meaningless:

> Enlarge my life with multitude of days,
> In health, in sickness, thus the suppliant prays;
> Hides from himself his state, and shuns to know,
> That life protracted is protracted woe.
> Time hovers o'er, impatient to destroy,
> And shuts up all the passages of joy:
> In vain their gifts the bounteous seasons pour,
> The fruit autumnal, and the vernal flow'r,
> With listless eyes the dotard views the store,
> He views, and wonders that they please no more:
> Now pall the tasteless meats, and joyless wines,
> And luxury with sighs her slave resigns.
> Approach, ye minstrels, try the soothing strain,
> Diffuse the tuneful lenitives of pain:
> No sounds alas would touch th' impervious ear,
> Though dancing mountains witness'd Orpheus near;
> Nor lute nor lyre his feeble pow'rs attend,
> Nor sweeter musick of a virtuous friend,
> But everlasting dictates croud his tongue,
> Perversely grave, or positively wrong.
> The still returning tale, and ling'ring jest,
> Perplex the fawning niece and pamper'd guest,

While growing hopes scarce awe the gath'ring sneer,
And scarce a legacy can bribe to hear;
The watchful guests still hint the last offence,
The daughter's petulance, the son's expence,
Improve his heady rage with treach'rous skill,
And mould his passions till they make his will.
    Unnumber'd maladies each joint invade,
Lay siege to life, and press the dire blockade;
But unextinguish'd av'rice still remains,
And dreaded losses aggravate his pains;
He turns, with anxious heart and cri'pled hands,
His bonds of debt, and mortgages of lands;
Or views his coffers with suspicious eyes,
Unlocks his gold, and counts it till he dies.

                              The Vanity of Human Wishes

Do we not see here that the wealth to which the human figure
has bound himself has thereby become a negative and destructive
principle? It obstructs the growth of maturity just as in Pope's
Timon's Villa the wealthy owner cannot really meet his guest in
an adult relationship. The accumulation of wealth represents the
possibility of satisfying desires but the price that the individual
has to pay is that the nature of these desires will become fixed,
able to expand only on a horizontal plane, as it were. You will be
limited to what money can buy and your desires will be multi-
plied quantitatively on this single level. It will be progressively
more difficult for the rich man to allow his desires to mature or to
change in quality. He will be possessed by his wealth. These are
only some of the implications of these two passages. Dr. Johnson
is not despising money; he had known poverty too well for that;
and his presentation of the bondage of anxiety and fear that great
possessions can bring is all the more impressive. 'Possessions bully
you, turn you into a generalization,' cried Birkin in D. H.
Lawrence's *Women in Love*. I think that Pope and Dr. Johnson
would in all seriousness have approved of these words.

One of the right uses of riches, then, and this will seem a paradox, may be the release of the individual self from a preoccupation
with possessions. To have enough will mean to have that which

will allow you to realize the possibilities of growth within yourself. There is a crucially relevant passage in James's *The Portrait of a Lady*. Mme. Merle is in conversation with Isabel Archer:

'When you've lived as long as I you'll see that every human being has his shell and that you must take the shell into account. By the shell I mean the whole envelope of circumstances. . . . What shall we call our 'self'? Where does it begin? Where does it end? It overflows into everything that belongs to us—and then it flows back again. I know a large part of myself is in the clothes I choose to wear. I've a great respect for *things*! One's self—for other people—is one's expression of one's self; and one's house, one's furniture, one's garments, the books one reads, the company one keeps—these things are all expressive.' This was very metaphysical. . . . Isabel was fond of metaphysics but was unable to accompany her friend into this bold analysis of human personality. 'I don't agree with you. I think just the other way. I don't know whether I succeed in expressing myself, but I know that nothing else expresses me. Nothing that belongs to me is any measure of me: everything's on the contrary a limit, a barrier, and a perfectly arbitrary one. Certainly the clothes which, as you say, I choose to wear, don't express me; and heaven forbid they should!'
'You dress very well,' Mme. Merle lightly interposed.
'Possibly: but I don't care to be judged by that. My clothes may express the dressmaker, but they don't express me. To begin with it's not my own choice that I wear them; they're imposed upon me by society.'
'Should you prefer to go without them?' Madame Merle enquired in a tone which virtually terminated the discussion.

In this particular instance, and the book as a whole will show convincingly what general validity can be given to it, the right use of riches is to place you in a situation so that you may be able to choose. How you choose will involve your own knowledge of yourself and the degree of maturity you have reached in your growth as an individual, and this itself is involved in the degree of health and maturity of civilization in the society in which you live. That is why there is no direct or simple answer to the question 'What is enough?' *The Portrait of a Lady* would provide one of the experiences out of which an answer might be constructed.

These hints and guesses may be brought to a close by offering a comment in the words of a writer who, though admired for a variety of reasons, not always for the relevant ones, has also been described as having the misfortune of lacking a tradition and being incapable of real thinking. I mean D. H. Lawrence. I do not propose to assess the quality of intelligence that Lawrence demonstrates in, for instance, *Women in Love*, but I will not hesitate in claiming that in what Lawrence writes of money—explicitly in the essays, and in dramatic representation in the novels—he is consciously or unconsciously sharing in a traditional wisdom which will include the morality *Everyman*, Jonson's *Volpone* and *The Alchemist* as well as the official teachings of the medieval church on this subject: 'Sometime—somewhere man will wake up and realize that possession is a kind of illness of the spirit, and a hopeless burden upon the spontaneous self.' 'An illness of the spirit': 'take physic, pomp'. Lear's cry is heard again.

Lawrence's fundamental criticism of modern societies is that, whatever they profess, they are all basically alike, concerned at heart with the acquisition of material possessions. They all assume that the ownership of things is the central human interest. '. . . socialism, conservatism, bolshevism, liberalism, republicanism, communism: all alike. The one principle that governs all the *isms* is the same; the principle of the idealized unit, the possession of property. Man has his highest fulfilment as a possessor of property: so they all say, really. One half says that the uneducated, being the majority, should possess the property; the other half say the educated, being the enlightened, should possess the property. There is no more to it. No need to consult books about it.' These words are from the essay entitled *Democracy*. A forcible assertion of the negative power of the love of money is made in his *Reflections on the Death of a Porcupine*: 'The golden wall of money—this is the fatal wall. It cuts off from life, from vitality, from the alive sun and the alive earth as nothing can. Nothing, not even the most fanatical dogmas of an iron-bound religion can insulate us from the inrush of life and inspiration as money can. . . . We are losing vitality owing to money and money standards.'

Can Lawrence help us towards an answer to the question 'What is enough, what is the just distribution?' 'The question of property,' he writes, 'will never be settled till people cease to care for property. . . . A man only needs so much as will help him to his own fulfilments. Surely the individual who wants a motor-car merely for the sake of having it and riding in it is as hopeless an automaton as the motor-car itself.' Lawrence's view of future possibilities of human growth restates the traditional and religious doctrine that the wealth of the world is not owned by men but should be used by them in their function as trustees and stewards (is it not significant that this word is predominantly associated nowadays with those necessary people who dispense alcohol in the saloons of liners and clubs or who have the last word in the affairs of horse-racing in this country?).

> ...When men are no longer obsessed with the desire to possess property, or with the parallel desire to prevent another man's possessing it, then, and only then, shall we be glad to turn it over to the State. . . . The Prime Minister of the future will be no more than a sort of steward, the Minister of Commerce will be the great housekeeper, the Minister for Transport the head-coachman; all just chief servants, no more: servants. . . .

> All settlement of the property question must arise spontaneously out of the new impulse in man to free himself from the extraneous load of possession, and walk naked and light. Every attempt at producing a new material world only adds another last straw to the load that already has broken so many backs. If we are to keep our backs unbroken, we must deposit all property on the ground, and learn to walk without it, we must stand aside. And when many men stand aside, they stand in a new world: a new world of man has come to pass. This is the Democracy: the new order.

When it was that Lawrence wrote these words is uncertain: the Essay from which they are taken was published in 1936, in *Phoenix*. They should command the respect of intelligent persons today. Our questions, though, have by no means been

answered. A man needs enough to help him to his own fulfilments. What is the nature of the fulfilments of each separate man
and woman has only been barely hinted at : but clearly this is our
central problem. The key words I offered at the beginning of this
essay were 'justice' and 'naturalness', but these are significant not
as abstractions but only as experienced in our own lives and in our
own fulfilments :

> The profoundest of all sensualities
> is the sense of truth
> and the next deepest sensual experience
> is the sense of justice.